Instructor's Manual with Test Bank for
Hatfield, Edwards, and Bitter

MATHEMATICS METHODS FOR ELEMENTARY AND MIDDLE SCHOOL TEACHERS

Third Edition

and Accompanying CD-ROM

Prepared by

Jean Morrow, Ed.D., O.S.M.

Emporia State University

Allyn and Bacon

Boston   London   Toronto   Sydney   Tokyo   Singapore

Preface

Activity and Ending Exercises Answers - Textbook

Extended Activity and Ending Exercises Answers - CD-ROM

Introduction to Section B - The CD-ROM   B-I.1

Introduction to Section C - Test Questions   C-I.1

Test Questions

Table of Contents

PREFACE TO THE THIRD EDITION

The instructor's manual is written in three sections:

SECTION A -- ACTIVITY AND ENDING EXERCISES ANSWERS from the TEXTBOOK

All of the textbook chapter activities, including the ending exercises for each chapter, are included in this section. Thus, each chapter 's ending exercises follow immediately after the activity exercises. Each answer is keyed to the text page where the original activity is presented. Since the video vignettes are found on the CD-ROM, any comments or remarks about the vignettes are found in Section B, the CD-ROM portion of the Instructor's Manual.

SECTION B -- EXTENDED ACTIVITY AND EXTENDED ENDING EXERCISES from the CD-ROM

As much as possible, answers for all the extended exercises that appear on the CD-ROM are keyed to a text page on which related material may have been introduced. Occasionally, the reference is to the CD-ROM itself. The ending exercises from both the text and the CD-ROM are identified by level of difficulty:

> A. MEMORIZATION and COMPREHENSION EXERCISES --
> Low-Level Thought Activities
> B. APPLICATION and ANALYSIS EXERCISES --
> Middle-Level Thought Activities
> C. SYNTHESIS and EVALUATION EXERCISES --
> High-Level Thought Activities

SECTION C -- TEST QUESTIONS

A test bank of questions is presented for each chapter in the text, and the pages are numbered to reflect each chapter at the bottom of the page. The pages can be removed from the instructor's manual to insure security if instructors wish to use the rest of the manual as a self-check for students.

Test questions have been field tested and categorized by their level of difficulty into low, medium, and high questions to correspond to the three levels of difficulty seen above in sections A and B. The questions are labeled L (low), M (medium), and H (high). Each question is coded by:

p 64   This tells the page in the text from which the test
       question
L(b)   was taken; it is a low level question whose answer is b.
       Answers have been randomized.

High level questions are labeled:

H(s) = <u>Students</u> create the answer but the question has only one
correct answer.

H(v) = Students create the answer but the answer will <u>vary</u> as in an
       essay question.

As in the second edition, several of the medium difficulty level
questions have been changed to the format used for the high
difficulty level questions. That is, some medium difficulty level
questions have this coding:

M(s) = <u>Students</u> create the answer but there is only one correct
       answer.
M(v) = Students create the answer but the answer <u>varies</u> as in an
       short-answer question.

Suggestions for alternative assessment at midterm and/or final
exam time can be found at the beginning of Section C.

The answer key immediately follows all the high-level questions
and a warning appears in the manual reminding the instructor to
cover up these answers when photocopying the test.

The answer key is at the left in such a way that a piece of paper
going down the side of the page can cover this information quickly
when photocopying questions for student test.

<u>Time Allotments for Test Items</u>

When preparing tests where the level of difficulty of questions vary,
the authors have found the following formula works well:

    Low level -- allow <u>1 minute</u> to answer per test item
    Medium level -- allow <u>2 minutes</u> to answer per test item
    High level -- allow 5-20 minutes to answer per test item,
            depending on the extent to which the student is
            asked to create a new solution.

Adding More Test Items

The activities and ending exercises within each chapter make excellent low level questions if students have done them alone outside of class and are tested for comprehension at exam time.

The activities and ending exercises make excellent medium level questions if they are extended by asking the learner to apply what has been learned in the chapter to a new situation.

Absent from the instructor's manual for this edition is a separate section for the computer-program questions. Since, for the most part those fall within the CD-ROM section of this edition, they are addressed in that section as they arise.   No spreadsheet program is included in this edition. It is anticipated that students would have access to a spreadsheet application either on their own personal computer or in a lab setting at their college or university. Students will have to refer to the manual for their particular application, if they do not already have a working knowledge of the spreadsheet, in order to create and explore the spreadsheet suggestions contained in this edition.

If you and/or your students do not have access to computers with a CD-ROM drive, and you would like to have the Turtle-LOGO demonstration program, send a blank disk with a stamped self-addressed disk mailer, specifying your preference for the IBM or Macintosh version, to

> Nancy Edwards, Ph.D.
> Missouri Western State College
> St. Joseph, MO 64507

and she will send you a copy of the demonstration program.

At the beginning of Section B, I share with you some of the pitfalls, frustrations, and new knowledge I gained as I attempted to use the CD-ROM for the first time. I was able to use it on both a Windows 95 system and a Macintosh system. Believe me, it was worth the learning pains to have so much additional material available for my methods students and myself.

+ + +

The authors hope you will enjoy the exciting and challenging experience of teaching mathematics in our day.

-- J. A. M.

ACTIVITY ANSWERS -- -- CHAPTER 1

COMPUTER ACTIVITY - - TEXT PAGE 14 ~~~~~~~~~ Scout
Report Subscriptions

Students are encouraged to "surf the net" first. Subscribing to a listserv may result in more mail than the student expects.

The "Integrating Technology" activities are noted in the CD-ROM section of this instructor's manual.

ENDING EXERCISES -- -- CHAPTER 1

A. MEMORIZATION and COMPREHENSION EXERCISES
Low-Level Thought Activities -- PAGE 20

1. Answers will vary. Among the more obvious differences that students might list are the generally increasing number of objectives, the addition of algebra in Gr. 5-8, the deletion of Concepts of Whole Number Operations in Gr. 5-8, Patterns and Relationships becomes Patterns and Functions, Fractions and Decimals is not a separate standard in Gr. 5-8, etc.

2. Students can check the math books in the college library with dates that correspond to the school days of their parents and grandparents as well as the students' own school days, for differences in content. Interviewing parents and grandparents will provide insights on the differences in methodology or pedagogy.

3. Answers will vary, depending on the futurist chosen.

4. Catalogs from commercial software companies can be the most efficient source for much of this information.

B. APPLICATION and ANALYSIS EXERCISES
Middle-Level Thought Activities -- PAGE 21

1. The aim is for the college student to see the cyclic nature of the changes in mathematics education. The title may change but the movement is essentially the same. For example . . .

Dates	Emphasis
a. 1910s	Mental discipline to handle new concepts
b. 1960s	New content & exploratory methods to deal with the Spating (Sputnik) aftermath
c. 1920s	Drill and practice
d. 1970s	Back to basics
e. 1930s	Development of insight, structure and patterns
f. 1980s	Development of problem solving

2. Answers will vary, depending on the journals chosen for the review.

C. SYNTHESIS and EVALUATION EXERCISES
High-Level Thought Activities -- PAGE 21

1. Answers will vary, but the positions can be based on the reading of one or more futurists (Exercise A, #3). The authors believe that there will still be a social aspect that will continue in meeting places, now called schools, and that there will be much greater individualization of assignments and programs of study using the Internet and other technologies.

2. Answers will vary, but the major thrust should refer to the studies that show calculator use produces better problem solvers and a more effective understanding of mathematical procedures.

3. Answers will vary, depending upon the software chosen.

4. The five goals of the NCTM curriculum standards are:
    a. Becoming a mathematical problem solver
    b. Learning to communicate mathematically
    c. Learning to reason mathematically
    d. Valuing mathematics
    e. Becoming confident in one's ability to do mathematics.

    Answers by the college students will vary on the importance of the goal in the students' future and how classroom instruction can help these goals.

5. Answers will vary. Reference to technological skills, problem solving abilities, and knowledge of the latest research in learning (e.g., brain theory, multiple intelligences) would be basic areas in which insights might be discussed.

ACTIVITY ANSWERS -- -- CHAPTER 2

```
**************************************************************
```
PLEASE NOTE: Questions to some of the problem solving activities on text pages 31-61 are answered in the text itself. Therefore, only activities where no answer is provided in the text will be shown here.
```
**************************************************************
```

ACTIVITY -- -- TEXT PAGE 32 ~~~~~~~~~~ Assessment of
Vygotsky's Constructivism

Answers will vary, but in general students should agree that Child 2 pushes his or her proximal development further during the lesson and yes, the teacher was wise in not asking the last question of Child 1. Child 1 had already indicated a degree of frustration ("too little to do anything with," "too many pieces" to make further questioning at this point profitable.

ACTIVITY -- -- TEXT PAGE 41 ~~~~~~~~~~ Creating EPRS for
Higher-Thought Activities

2. Presumably the college student will be able to list all of the basic facts that add to 7. The possible combinations beyond the basic facts are infinite and include the use of negative numbers, fractional numbers, and decimals.

3. Answer will vary but could include such suggestions as, "I'm going to give you one pair of addends and I want you to use those same addends in a different order to create the same sum as the original pair."

ACTIVITY -- -- TEXT PAGE 48 ~~~~~~~~~~ Creating Your Own
Problem-Solving Story from Cultural Folktales

Answers will vary depending upon the stories chosen.

ACTIVITY -- -- TEXT PAGE 51 ~~~~~~~~~~ Looking for Patterns
with the Peg Puzzle (Example 1)

# of Pairs (x)	# of Moves (y)	Pattern to See
1	3	$3x = y$
2	8	$4x = y$
3	15	$5x = y$
4	24	$6x = y$
5	35	$7x = y$

General Formula for All Cases: $x(x + 2) = y$

ACTIVITY -- -- TEXT PAGE 51 ~~~~~~~~~~ Looking for Patterns
with Regions of a Circle (Example 2)

# of Points	# of Regions
1	1
2	2
3	4
4	8
5	16
6	30

ACTIVITY -- -- TEXT PAGE 52 ~~~~~~~~~~ Drawing Tables
(Example 2)

The formula for finding the average for each player is (Game 1 +
Game 2 + Game 3)/3.

ACTIVITY -- -- TEXT PAGE 52 ~~~~~~~~~~ Elimination of
Extraneous Data

The fact that Rambo is a 35-pound dog does not affect the price of
the dog food. It is the extraneous data.

ACTIVITY -- -- TEXT PAGE 53 ~~~~~~~~~~ Working Backwards
(Example 1)

1. When parallel lines are cut by a transversal, angle x and angle y
   are the same number of degrees.
2. A straight line = 180 degrees.
3. When a straight line is bisected by a line forming two angles, the
   formula is:

   $180^O - 120^O$ = angle y

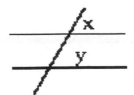

   therefore, angle y = 60°

<u>ACTIVITY -- -- TEXT PAGE 53</u> ~~~~~~~~~~ Working Backwards
(Example 2)

The common element is the big room. If the big room is 1/2 the

load, it can be visualized as seen in the left diagram below: 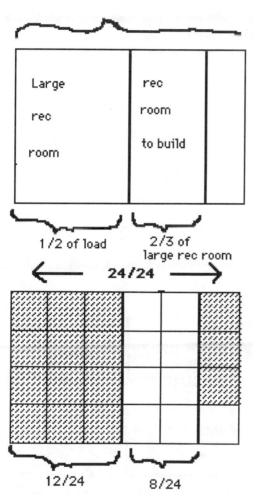 =

part to give back

Therefore, 2/3 of the 1/2 is 2/6 of the total load or 1/3 of the total
load is needed to build the rec room. If one gives back 5/8 of the
load, will it be more or less than the 1/3 of the load needed to build
the room? The common denominator of 5/8 and 1/3 is twenty-
fourths. See the diagram above. Therefore,

$1/3 = 8/24$ and $5/8 = 15/24$

Hence, the solution is:

24/24 total - 15/24 to give back = 9/24 left

One needs 8/24; so there will be 1/24 more left over than needed to do the job. Hence, 5/8 of the load can be given back to the lumber yard.

ACTIVITY -- -- TEXT PAGE 53 ~~~~~~~~ Flowcharting

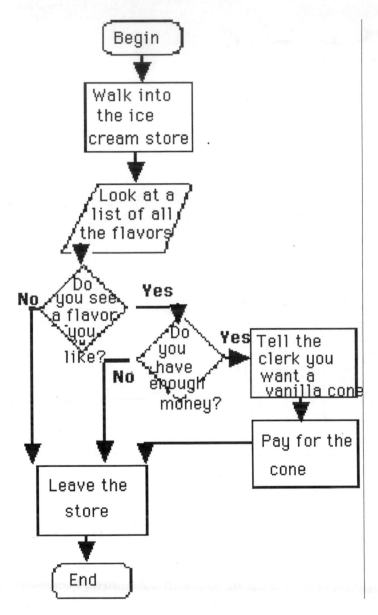

ACTIVITY -- -- TEXT PAGE 54 ~~~~~ Acting out the Problem
The sum of groceries for the three customers if $7.50. The total dollar value, if the same amount is sold for four days, is $30.00.

ACTIVITY -- -- TEXT PAGE 57 ~~~~~ Portfolio Assessment
2. Good arguments can be made for "working backwards," eliminating extraneous information and making a

table/chart/graph. Evidence of eliminating extraneous information is the crossing out of non-essential information; the evidence of working backwards is inferred in the placement of Mateo and Red Cloud on their appropriate lines. Some would consider the repeated lines and stick figures as a type of chart; others would call it drawing a picture. A strategy not named in the text that some would use to label this approach is "logical reasoning."

4. There are several scoring rubrics the student could use, particularly text page 110; Figure 4.4, page 112, Figure 4.6; or page 118, Figure 4.10.

ACTIVITY -- -- TEXT PAGE 61 ~~~~~~~~~~LOGO Activities

3. The "Free Explore" program would generally foster higher-level thought as students attempted to make the turtle do certain moves or create particular shapes. One possibility changing the *Add* program to enhance higher-level cognition would be to have the computer display one pair of addends and then the student is to enter a second, different, pair of addends that has the same sum.

ENDING EXERCISES -- -- CHAPTER 2

A. MEMORIZATION and COMPREHENSION EXERCISES
Low-Level Thought Activities -- PAGE 62

1. a. Looking for patterns
   b. Developing formulas and writing equations
   c. Modeling by constructing and manipulating the shapes
2. Answers will vary. The EPR might include the use of dominoes, number tiles, number sentence strips, or similar materials, as well as slateboards or flashcards.

B. APPLICATION and ANALYSIS EXERCISES
Middle-Level Thought Activities -- PAGE 62

1. Answers will vary, depending on the elementary or middle school textbook page chosen.
2. This question blends the knowledge covered in text for the elaborating technique and for the problem solving strategies.

Answers will vary, depending on the strategy and dialogue chosen by the college student.
3. Answers will vary depending upon the grade level, textbook, and word problems selected by the student.

C. SYNTHESIS and EVALUATION EXERCISES
High-Level Thought Activities -- PAGE 62

1. The creation of the lesson plan is presented here to integrate all the points discussed in the chapter which go into an effective mathematics lesson. The student should respond to points *a* through *k*.
2. Answers will vary depending upon the teaching scene chosen. The essential element is the guiding towards, rather than the telling of, an appropriate mathematical conclusion.

ACTIVITY ANSWERS -- -- CHAPTER 3

ACTIVITY -- -- TEXT PAGE 73 ~~~~~~~~~~ Creating Your Own
Numeration System

Portfolio Reflection: The college student should recognize that
Teisha chose 6000 as the significant numeral here since any number
in the 5000's enables her to use the circle as representative of 5 of
"what's inside." What Teisha fails to recognize is that numbers
such as those between 2000 and 5000 will call for longer symbols
than Mary's.

ACTIVITY -- -- TEXT PAGE 77 ~~~~~~~~~~ Finding the Next
Mayan Number

13 & 14 are

60 & 80 are the ellipse with 2 pairs of lines inside and 3 and 4 dots
respectively above the "eye."

ACTIVITY -- -- TEXT PAGE 79 ~~~~~~~~~~ Cooking up Metrics
with Hispanic American Recipes

No answers are required here.

ACTIVITY -- -- TEXT PAGE 80 ~~~~~~~~~~ Hindu Problem Solving
from India

There are 4 items that can be picked up with the first hand, 3 for the
second, 2 for the third, and 1 for the final hand. That makes a total
of 4 x 3 x 2 x 1 or 24 total ways to pick up the four items.

ACTIVITY -- -- TEXT PAGE 81 ~~~~~~~~~~ Creating a New
Counting Book Like Anno Did

No answers are required here.

ACTIVITY -- -- TEXT PAGE 83 ~~~~~~~~~~ Women in
                                              Mathematics

No answers are required here.

ACTIVITY -- -- TEXT PAGE 85 ~~~~~~~~~~ Number Patterns

No answers are required here.

ACTIVITY -- -- TEXT PAGE 88 ~~~~~~~~~~ The Discovery
                                    Approach and the Storytelling Approach

No answers are required here.

ENDING EXERCISES -- -- CHAPTER 3

A. MEMORIZATION and COMPREHENSION EXERCISES
Low-Level Thought Activities -- PAGE 95

1. 3 areas of research: <u>Impact of technology, the development of problem solving and critical thinking, the use of cultural qualities to help mathematics equity for all students</u> which attempt to answer these questions in particular: <u>How can we take students from culturally-diverse backgrounds and give them the mathematical understanding needed to be full participants in society? How much does the presence of diverse cultural backgrounds and beliefs play in the acquisition of mathematics understanding?</u>

2. Answers will vary, depending on the textbook series selected.

B. APPLICATION and ANALYSIS EXERCISES
Middle-Level Thought Activities -- PAGE 95

1. Answers will vary, depending on the material chosen in Exercise A - 2.
2. Answers will vary, depending upon the sources used and topics chosen.

3. Answers will vary, but students should look for examples other than those already cited in the text. A by-product of this exercise will be the realization that many of the older history of mathematics texts devote their pages almost exclusively to European males.

C. SYNTHESIS and EVALUATION EXERCISES
High-Level Thought Activities -- PAGE 96

1. Answers will vary, depending on the lesson chosen. The points listed, however, should be included in the plan.

2. Answers will vary, depending on the classroom visited.

3. Materials prepared for this activity will vary depending on the site, grade level, and topics addressed in the tutoring sessions.

4. Among the techniques that students might describe are: (1) collecting a file of activities/information that can be used to introduce the contributions of different cultures at appropriate times; (2) celebrate the contributions of different cultures; (3) integrate mathematics and social studies in appropriate and meaningful ways; (5) use appropriate children's literature; (6) use technology for applying/developing logical and critical reasoning skills; present materials in both field-dependent and field-independent settings; (7) use scaffolding and modeling to support children's oral discourse about mathematics; (8) be conscious of language barriers for LEP students; (9) be sensitive to scenarios developed as "real world" situations; and (10) use theory building and criticism to develop generalized procedures and conceptual thinking.

ACTIVITY -- -- TEXT PAGE 108 ~~~~~~~~~ Smoking and Cancer

The instructor may choose to substitute a topic important to your state interests.

In terms of each student evaluating the group's work, you may suggest they keep notes on some or all of the following:
Did the group interact well?
What strategies did the group employ to complete this task?
What mathematics did the group employ?
How well did the group explaintheir methods and communicate their findings? to each other? to the class?
What was the group's attitude toward this task?

Or, you may give them a checklist with such criteria as:
Shows initiative
Shows leadership
Explains ideas clearly
Adaptable/flexible
Organizes tasks efficiently
Values accuracy
Shows perseverance
Offers assistance appropriately
Accepts assistance appropriately
Accepts and abides by a group decision
Thoughtfully considers the ideas of others

ACTIVITY -- -- TEXT PAGE 109 ~~~~~~~~~ Modeling Numbers

No answers are required here.

ACTIVITY -- -- TEXT PAGE 111 ~~~~~~~~~ Interviews about Mathematics

No answers are required here.

ACTIVITY -- -- TEXT PAGE 112 ~~~~~~~~~~ Mysterious Money
                                        Problem

No answers are required here.

ACTIVITY -- -- TEXT PAGE 112 ~~~~~~~~~~ Taxman Game

No answers are required here.

ACTIVITY -- -- TEXT PAGE 113 ~~~~~~~~~~ Show You Know How

No answers are required here.

ENDING EXERCISES -- -- CHAPTER 4

A. MEMORIZATION and COMPREHENSION EXERCISES
Low-Level Thought Activities -- PAGE 120

1. Alternative assessment is "consistent with curriculum goals,
    embedded in real-world situations, and encompasses a number
    of procedures for observing, collecting, and evaluationg student
    learning." (See pp. 105-6 for further characteristics.) Examples of
    assessment tools include interviews, observations, questioning
    (i.e., open-ended, higher order thinking), performance tasks,
    portfolios, group projects, etc.

2. The six criteria are found on page 107 in the text.

3. Those areas that should receive less attention according to the
    NCTM documents can be found on page 105 in the text.

4. Among the reasons that students might cite for parents opposing
    alternative testing are: concern that not enough emphasis is
    given to "basics" so their students can perform well on
    standardized tests; seeing no purpose to open-ended questions ...
    "How can you count that wrong when you ask them to explain
    how they found their answer?"; not knowing what "grade" is
    associated with each rating on the rubric; penalizing "my child
    who did all his/her part of the assignment" because the group
    did not do well on their project assignment; "I can't help my
    child study for this kind of test;" concern that this is just another

educational fad; "what does writing have to do with mathematics?"; etc.

B. APPLICATION and ANALYSIS EXERCISES
Middle-Level Thought Activities -- PAGE 121

1. Student explanations might include "pre-standards" thinking such as "teaching to the (standardized) test." An example of this is teaching an algorithm out of context because it's "on the test." Other explanations might include the idea that we test what we value, and so if we value problem solving in cooperative group settings, we will test problem solving in cooperative group settings. Another explanation might include the idea that if there are state mandated or district mandated tests that teachers teach a curriculum that meets the concepts/topics/areas being assessed.

2. Student responses may include the following ideas: Standardized tests are, generally speaking, used for one of four purposes: ranking or sorting students; reporting on program effectiveness; comparing teachers, schools, and/or districts; and making policy decisions. They are generally top-heavy with computation and estimation. They are norm-referenced. It should be noted that if used as <u>one</u> source of data in program evaluation or student progress there is a place for standardized tests. It should also be noted that standardized tests are not usually in alignment with a district's curriculum. Alternative assessments, on the other hand, are usually closely aligned with the district curriculum; they are embedded in instruction, highlight the usefulness of mathematical thinking, evaluate the entire problem solving process. Alternative assessments are aligned with student outcomes and classroom instruction; are ongoing and value informed teacher judgment; are composed of meaningful and worthwhile tasks; provide a source of useful information for instructional decisions; and involve the students in the assessment process.

3. Responses will vary depending on textbooks and ancillary materials that are perused.

C. SYNTHESIS and EVALUATION EXERCISES
High-Level Thought Activities -- PAGE 121

1. Answers will vary.

2. Again, answers will vary but should include many of the ideas about alternative assessment developed in question 2, part B.

3. Answers will vary depending upon the task(s) chosen.

ACTIVITY ANSWERS -- -- CHAPTER 5

ACTIVITY -- -- TEXT PAGE 131 ~~~~~~~~~~ Solids Exploration

1. Eight shapes can become a box without a lid:
B C D F G H J K
(See the Pentomino Activity--Text Page 142)

2. A sheet 5x4 will make four topless boxes if cut like this:

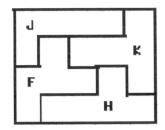

4. The containers pictured on page 131 are the artist's conception. The activity should be done with **real** containers. The intention is:

A and D ⎫ will hold the   C and F will hold the least.

C and F ⎭ same amount.   E will hold the most.

ACTIVITY -- TEXT PAGE 132 ~~~~~~~~~~ Change it and Describe it

The area may change. The perimeter will remain the same since you are working with a fixed length.

ACTIVITY -- TEXT PAGE 132 ~~~~~~~~~~ One- and Two-Difference
Trains

Answers will vary depending on the first piece chosen. Examples are given in the procedure for this activity.

ACTIVITY -- -- TEXT PAGE 228 ~~~~~~~~~~ Using a Geoboard

Included here are samples of some responses to activities suggested.

Make This Shape

Smallest shape   Largest shape

Rubber band lifted and stretched around another nail: (The original small triangle is sketched as a dotted line.)
Some possibilities: A figure with 5 corners:

Dividing Our Shapes
Largest shape divided into congruent areas:

Triangles   Rectangles

One of the above regions divided again: Triangle   Square

... plus other possibilities can be seen
if the geoboard has been rotated.

How Am I Classifying
Answers will vary. See page 134 of the text for an example.

ACTIVITY -- -- TEXT PAGE 134 ~~~~~~~~~~ Roll a Triangle

Not all combinations will build triangles. There are 216 possible outcomes of which 111 will build a triangle. The 33 different combinations are (1,1,1), (1,2,2), (1,3,3), (1,4,4), (1,5,5), (1,6,6), (2,2,2), (2,2,3), (2,3,3), (2,3,4), (2,4,4), (2,4,5), (2,5,5), (2,5,6), (3,3,3), (3,3,4), (3,3,5), (3,4,4), (3,4,5), (3,4,6), (3,5,5), (3,5,6), (3,6,6), (4,4,4), (4,4,5), (4,4,6), (4,5,5), (4,5,6), (4,6,6), (5,5,5), (5,5,6), (5,6,6), (6,6,6). There are 6 equilateral triangles, 20 isosceles triangles, and 7 scalene triangles in these 33 different combinations. If you consider all possible 111 combinations there are 6 equilateral triangles, 63 isosceles triangles, and 42 scalene triangles.
The sum of lengths of any two sides must be greater than the length of the third side.
There can be at most one obtuse angle.

ACTIVITY -- -- TEXT PAGE 135 ~~~~~~~~~~ Using Tangrams

1. Similar Shapes

   The triangles

   Congruent Shapes
   Pair One: 2 small triangles

   Pair Two: 2 large triangles

2. Two small triangles
   can become: Congruent with:
   a square   the square
   a triangle   the medium triangle
   a parallelogram   the parallelogram

3. Squares (6): 2 large triangles; 2 small triangles; a large triangle, 2 small triangles, and the parallelogram; a large triangle, 2 small triangles, and the square; the square, a medium triangle, 2 small triangles, and the parallelogram; a medium triangle and 2 small triangles.

4. The two large congruent triangles can form a parallelogram, a square, and an isosceles triangle.

Here are examples of the number of tangrams needed to make different shapes.

	Number of Tangrams Used					
Shape	2	3	4	5	6	7
Triangle	x	x				
Rectangle		x		x		
Trapezoid		x				
Parallelogram		x				
Square	x	x	x	x	x	x

6. All of the alphabet letters and numbers can be made in some stylized form.

ACTIVITY -- -- TEXT PAGE 136 ~~~~~~~~~ Can You Picture This?

This activity is similar to "Can You Build it?" on text page 129. Both activities help to build skill in mathematical communication, by encouraging use of correct terminology, relative position, and visualization.

ACTIVITY -- -- TEXT PAGE 137 ~~~~~~~~~ Symmetry in Letters
                                            and Words

The letters with rotational symmetry are:
        H I N O S X Z   (A half turn will produce the same figure.)
A circle has an infinite number of lines of symmetry.

ACTIVITY -- -- TEXT PAGE 139 ~~~~~~~~~ Video Vignette

See the CD-ROM Section of the Instructor's Manual.

ACTIVITY -- -- TEXT PAGE 142 ~~~~~~~~~ Pentominoes

1. All pentominoes have the same area, 5 square units.
    All but one pentomino has the same perimeter, p = 12 units.
    The exception is L with a perimeter of 10 units.

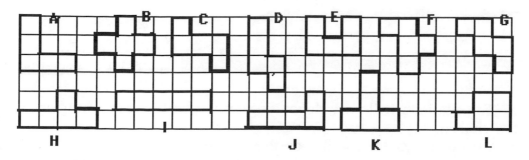

By changing one edge at a time and flipping, sliding, and rotating each new arrangement, the pentominoes (shown above) are the only 12 arrangements that are not repetitions.

2. Those that can be folded into a cube without a lid:

    B C D F G H J K

    When looking at each one it is apparent that every fold permits you to move into an area that is not occupied. This is not true for the other four pentominoes.

3. Yes, a 6 x 10 rectangle can be formed. Yes, a 5 x 12 rectangle can be formed. Yes, there are other rectangles that can be formed as long as the length and width multiplied together equals 60 square units because all of the 12 pentominoes taken together have an area of 60 square units.

    Other possibilities include:

    3 x 20 rectangle   4 x 15 rectangle

4. No, a 2 x 5 rectangle, using different pentominoes, is not possible. For a 3 x 5 rectangle, some possibilities follow:

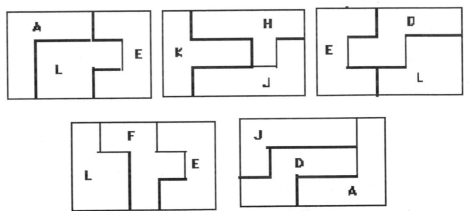

    A 4x5 rectangle can be made using four different pentominoes with variations possible.

    A 5x5 rectangle can be made using 5 different pentominoes with many variations. The patterns goes up to a 12x5 rectangle with all 12 pentominoes being used.

Some possibilities:

	3x5 rectangle	4x5 rectangle	
Pentominoes	A E L	G H J L	A C J L
Used	H J K	A D I J	E F H J
	D E L	A E F J	H I J K
	A D J	D E I L	A G J K

5. Tessellations will vary depending on which two pentominoes are chosen.

6. Various plays are possible on the checkerboard.

ACTIVITY -- -- TEXT PAGE 143 ~~~~~~~~~~ Discovering Area with
                                             Tangrams

1. The area of the triangle is 1/2 (one-half) square unit.
2. The area of the parallelogram is the same as the 2 triangles when
   they are in the shape of a square. Therefore, the area of the
   parallelogram is 1 square unit.
3. The area of the square is 2 sq. units. All of the areas are 2 sq.
   units; only the perimeters change.

same perimeter

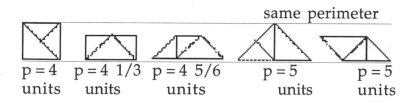

p = 4   p = 4 1/3 p = 4 5/6   p = 5   p = 5
units   units   units   units   units

from least to greatest perimeter

4. Based on the same unit measurements as those above, all the
   areas below are 4 sq. units. The perimeters are shown from least
   to greatest.

same perimeter

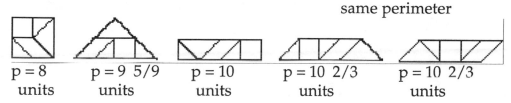

p = 8   p = 9 5/9   p = 10   p = 10 2/3   p = 10 2/3
units   units   units   units   units

from least to greatest perimeter

5. All of the shapes in #4 have the greatest area = 4 sq. units. The
   last two figures in #4 have the greatest perimeter.

6. If the square formed by the seven tangram pieces has a total area
   of one, then the area of the individual pieces is as follows:
   Large triangles -- 1/4 sq. unit each
   Medium triangle -- 1/8 sq. unit
   Small triangles -- 1/16 sq. unit each
   Square -- 1/8 sq. unit
   Parallelogram -- 1/8 sq. unit
Fractional, decimal, and ratio/proportional relationships may be
   determined accordingly.

<u>ACTIVITY -- -- TEXT PAGE 143</u> ~~~~~~~~~~ Exploring Area and
Perimeter with Geoboards

1. This perimeter = 4 units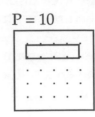
2. Figures with a perimeter of:

   P = 4   P = 6   P = 7   P = 10

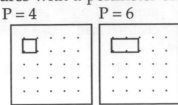

cannot be done
with rt. angles

Examples with perimeters of 8:

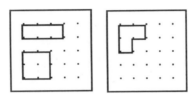

3. = 1 square unit of area - Other squares are seen in the
following problems.

4. Figures of different perimeters and area:

   P = 12   P = 8   P = 12   P = 10
   A = 9   A = 4   A = 8   A = 4

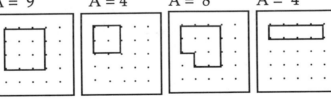

5. Area of triangle = .5 sq. unit
   Area of small squares = 1 sq. unit each
   Area of large square = 2 sq. units
   The relationship: 1 s.u. + 1 s.u. = 2 s.u.

6. Yes, the relationship is the same as the rectangles in step 5.

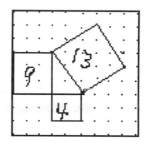

Areas were 9 s.u. ⎸ 4 s.u. – 13 s.u.

7. If MN is the hypotenuse, the right triangle drawn would legs of
   1 unit and 2 units with the area of the squares:

   1 s.u. + 4 s.u. = 5 s.u. as the area of the square with MN as its
   side.

8. Square units in the three figures:

   7 sq. units   8 sq. units   8 sq. units

ACTIVITY -- -- TEXT PAGE 144 ~~~~~~~~~~ Additional Activities
                                       for Area with Geoboards

1. In 1 square unit of area, there are 4 nails touching and no nails
   inside.
2. The area is 1.5 sq. units with 5 nails touching and no nails inside.
   The area is 2 sq. units with 6 nails touching and no nails inside.
   The table develops:

A	T	I
1	4	0
1.5	5	0
2	6	0
2.5	7	0

3. The area increases by one-half as touching nails increase by one.
   The prediction is that the pattern will hold as long as the nails
   inside remain constant at zero.
4. See the table above in #2.
5. Some examples are shown below.

A	T	I
1	4	0
2	4	1
3	4	2
4	4	3

As the nails inside increase by one, the area also increases by one when the touching nails remain constant at four.

6. A function using the two variables of area to inside nails is: A = I + 1

7. Area of the rectangle = 6 sq. units.   The area of the triangle = 3 sq. units.

8. The answer is explained in the exercise.

9. Area of the rectangle = 6 sq. units.

The parallelogram has a base of 3 and a height of 2. Its area is 2 x 3 = 6 sq. units.

10. The formula is: A = T/2 + I - 1

ACTIVITY -- -- TEXT PAGE 145 ~~~~~~~~~~ What is the Figure?

1. The coordinate pairs made   2. The coordinate pairs made
        this figure: this figure:

3. Answers will vary.

ENDING EXERCISES -- -- CHAPTER 5

A. MEMORIZATION and COMPREHENSION EXERCISES
Low-Level Thought Activities -- PAGE 148

1. Answers may vary somewhat, depending on the textbook series chosen, but the properties of solids must include information about the sides, angles, length, width, height, and the formula relationship of each one as it relates to its volume.

2. Answers will vary, but all answers should include justification for the restructuring of the developmental sequence of geometric topics. The college student should indicate examples of geometric objects as seen by the topological view and the Euclidean view so the instructor sees that the student has a clear idea of the two topics and how children will answer questions when such topics are presented in geometry.

3. The college student needs to sketch geoboard examples like those found on text page 144, points 7, 8, 9, and 10. The explanation for finding the area of both figures should be in the student's own words, using precise language from which the formulas could be derived.

B. APPLICATION and ANALYSIS EXERCISES
Middle-Level Thought Activities -- PAGE 148

1-2. Answers will vary, but each point should be supported by clear justifications based on the concepts and research covered in this chapter.

3-4. Answers will vary, depending on the teaching materials and topics chosen for each of these activities.

C. SYNTHESIS and EVALUATION EXERCISES
High-Level Thought Activities -- PAGE 149

1. } All of these activities ask students to plan lessons
2. } for a particular subject or grade level dealing with geometry. The Chicago Mathematics Instruction Process lesson plan form (found on the CD-ROM in Chapter 2) is recommended as the plan of choice when developing the lessons.

3. The beginning student of Logo who wishes to do the Logo activity outlined here may find the *Turtle Math* demo helpful. Activities will vary.

4. In addition to suggestions in the text and on the CD-ROM, a search of the internet will provide many possible activities that the student can develop that in geometry that incorporate multicultural linkages.

ACTIVITY ANSWERS -- -- CHAPTER 6

<u>ACTIVITY -- -- TEXT PAGE 156</u> ~~~~~~~~~ Creating Your Own
Need for Standard Measurement Tools

2. Some ways to measure the length and width of your desk using
your body:
a. forearm
b. hand
c. index finger   {Answers will vary; these are only examples.}
d. foot
e. entire arm
7. e.g., finger tip to the first joint

<u>ACTIVITY -- -- TEXT PAGE 158</u> ~~~~~~~~~ Guessing Metric
Measurement

1. A person's height compared to arm span:
   A person's arm span is approximately 40% as long as the
   person's height. This was true when measuring people from 23
   months to 80 years of age for this sample.

2-5. These measurements will vary depending on the weight
        of the individual.
6. An example of one possible bar graph representing different
    lengths of each body part (to the nearest centimeter):

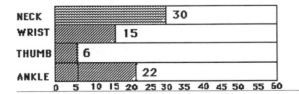

Lengths of Body Parts in Centimeters

<u>ACTIVITY -- -- TEXT PAGE 160</u> ~~~~~~~~~ Estimation with Large
Measures

Answers will vary. A meter stick or a meter wheel with a long
handle is best for measuring large areas where walking is required.

<u>ACTIVITY -- -- TEXT PAGE 161</u> ~~~~~~~~~ Weight with Foil Boats

Answers will vary. In general, the fewer heavy objects the longer
the boat will stay afloat. (Is there a point at which enough lighter

weight objects will have the same result as the heavier objects, i.e. causing the boat to sink?)

ACTIVITY -- -- TEXT PAGE 163 ~~~~~~~~~ Finding Mass with a
Balance in Science

Answers will vary but estimates should improve if the activity is done more than once.

ACTIVITY -- -- TEXT PAGE 164 ~~~~~~~~~ Mass with Silver
Dollars

1. A kilogram is 1000 grams. Therefore, 1000 grams divided by 18 grams (the mass of one silver dollar) would give you $55.55 or 55 silver dollars plus . . . half the mass of the next silver dollar. As a proportion:

$$\frac{1000 \text{ grams}}{18 \text{ grams}} = \frac{x}{\$1.00}$$
$$18x = \$1000$$
$$x = \$55.55$$

2. If one silver dollar is 18 grams, 1000 silver dollars would be 18 x 1000 = 18,000 grams as the mass.
3. Answers will vary as students perform this task.
4. The same steps as those above using a nickel in place of the silver dollar:

A nickel's mass is 10 grams.
Answers to steps 1-3 using the nickel . . .
a. 1000/10 = 100 nickels or $5.00
b. The mass of 1000 nickels is 10,000 grams.
c. Answers will vary depending on the mass of each student.

ACTIVITY -- -- TEXT PAGE 166 ~~~~~~~~~ Exploring
Circumference and Diameter

1. PLEASE NOTE: Measurements of commercial cans will differ slightly in Canada and other countries using the metric system.

Object	C	D	C+D	C/D	C-D	CxD
(reported in cm) Soda can (12 oz; 354 mL)	21	6.6	27.6	3.181	14.4	138.6
Coffee can (1 lb size)	32.1	10.2	42.3	3.147	21.9	327.42

Plate Glass Waste-basket		Answers	will vary and	with shape	the chosen.	size

2. Column 4, C/D, on the preceding chart shows the constant relationship between circumference and diameter.
3. The average value of C/D should be close to 3.14.
4. It is the constant known as Pi.

ACTIVITY -- -- TEXT PAGE 166 ~~~~~~~~~~ With Centimeter Graph Paper

Answers will vary depending on the size of the students' hands/feet.

ACTIVITY -- -- TEXT PAGE 168 ~~~~~~~~~~ Cubic Centimeters

After the cubic centimeter container has been made, the experiment can be set up as follows:
1. Weigh the container you made <u>first without</u> any water.
2. Use paper clips on one side of an equal arm balance to see how many grams the container weighs when placed on the other side of the scale.
3. Add the gram of water to the container.
4. You should only need to add one paper clip (#1 silverette clip-- standard size) to the other side to balance the scale.
5. Therefore, one mL = one gram.

ACTIVITY -- -- TEXT PAGE 169 ~~~~~~~~~~ Comparing Volumes and Capacities

Steps 1-7 give the directions to set up the experiment on text page 169.

<u>WARNING</u> -- Encourage students to use dry materials that can be SOLIDLY PACKED, such as sand and <u>unpopped</u> popcorn. Popped popcorn and dry cereal with flakes that vary in size will not give accurate results.

8. When sand and unpopped popcorn are used (where the grains and kernels are more solidly packed), the mass is at the same level for each material when switched to the wide container.

9. One example of measuring the contents of each tube is shown below. The volume is:

Formula: $\pi\, r^2 h$
Tall cylinder: 3.14 (1.9)^2 15.5 cm = 175.6987 cm^3
Wide cylinder: 3.14 (3.1)^2 5.8 cm = 175.01732 cm^3

Notice: The volume is the same (as close as can be expected given the imprecision of measurement when using common metric rulers).

ACTIVITY -- -- TEXT PAGE 170 ~~~~~~~~~~ Building Cubes

| | | # of Blocks | |
Cube 1	L x W x H	on one edge	Volume
1	1 x 1 x 1	1	1
2	2 x 2 x 2	4	8
3	3 x 3 x 3	9	27
4	4 x 4 x 4	16	64
5	5 x 5 x 5	25	125

The pattern:
As each cube grows larger, any one of its sides s, taken to the third power, equals the volume.

A generalized formula for the volume of a cube:
$V = s^3$ or $V = L \times W \times H$

ACTIVITY -- -- TEXT PAGE 170 ~~~~~~~~~~ Using Formulas

1. The volume of the cylinder = 7694.45 cm^3
The volume of the cone = 1285.57 cm^3
The volume of the sphere = 10,531.38 cm^3

2. The volume of the cylinder is . . .
a. when the height is doubled = 2442.68 cm^3
b. when the radius is doubled = 4885.36 cm^3
c. when the radius and the height are doubled = 97703.73 cm^3
d. when the height is halved = 610.67 cm^3
e. when the height and the radius are halved = 252.67 cm^3
f. when the radius and height are multiplied by 5 = 152,667.59 cm^3

3. The volume of the cone is . . .
a. when the height is doubled = 2571.14 cm^3
b. when the radius is doubled = 5142.27 cm^3
c. when the radius and the height are doubled = 10,284.55 cm^3

d. when the height is halved = <u>642.78 cm^3</u>
e. when the height and the radius are halved = <u>160.70 cm^3</u>
f. when the radius and height are multiplied by 5 = <u>160,696.04 cm^3</u>

The volume of the sphere is . . .
     PLEASE NOTE: Height is not a relevant measure. Therefore: a, c, and d are omitted.
b. when the radius is doubled = <u>84,251.01 cm^3</u>
e. when the height and the radius are halved = <u>1316.42 cm^3</u>
f. when the radius and height are multiplied by 5 = <u>1,316,422.0 cm^3</u>

<u>ACTIVITY -- -- TEXT PAGE 171</u> ~~~~~~~~~ Simultaneous
                                           Comparisons

When two different size balls drop simultaneously from the same height (without a push), they will reach the floor at the same time regardless of their size or weight. Only differences in surface texture would effect their fall through the air.

To generalize the observation, different size balls can be used. The observation remains the same with each set of balls chosen, as was first reported at the leaning Tower of Pisa by Galileo and his colleagues.

<u>Note</u>: Children frequently measure the bounce back up instead of the time the balls reach the floor. The level to which the balls bounce back will differ with their resiliency. It is important for children NOT to confuse the two processes.

<u>ACTIVITY -- -- TEXT PAGE 171</u> ~~~~~~~~~ Use of the Egg Timer
                                           in Science

Answers will vary depending on:
1. The physical activity used with the egg timer, and
2. the design of the new timer

<u>ACTIVITY -- -- TEXT PAGE 172</u> ~~~~~~~~~ Using a Pendulum

1. Directions are found on text page 172.
2. Ways to change the beat of a pendulum:
      a. Start the swing from farther out, creating a wider arc to the swing.
      b. Start the swing from a near-center position, creating a short arc to the swing.
      c. Make the string shorter.

    d. Make the string longer, holding the string at its endpoint.

3. For a pendulum to swing twice as often, it must start from a distance as short as the other pendulum. A wrist watch with a second hand can be used to measure the swing of both pendulums.
4. Answers will vary depending on the length of the room. The second hand on a wrist watch may be used as the timing device.

ACTIVITY --- TEXT PAGE 173 ~~~~~~~~~ Experiments with
                                               Temperature

      Customary System
      Body temperature 98.6 degrees F
      Freezing point of water 32 degrees F
      Room temperature 72-74 degrees F
      Boiling point of water 212 degrees F

      Metric System
      Body temperature 54,8 degrees C
      Freezing point of water 0 degrees F
      Room temperature 40-41 degrees C
      Boiling point of water 100 degrees C

ACTIVITY -- -- TEXT PAGE 174 ~~~~~~~~~ Making Clocks

Explanation and directions for the activity appear on text pages 174-175.

ACTIVITY -- -- TEXT PAGE 175 ~~~~~~~~~ Portfolio Assessments

Answers will vary somewhat but such considerations as time elapsed, a.m. and p.m., number of minutes in an hour, number of days in a week as related to time itself would be part of the rubric. In addition, students need a basic understanding of subtraction and multiplication (or repeated addition). Knowing a.m. and p.m. is not as crucial in these problems, and should be given a lesser weight.

Since these are not open-ended questions, students may find it easier to develop a rubric in more of a checklist format, listing the facets or elements of mathematics needed to successfully perform the given operation. The various rating categories might be: competent (complete understanding - 5), needs improvement (partial understanding - 3), not yet (no answer, no understanding - 0). Credit should be given for this part if the college student identifies the essential components of the task, with adequate descriptors.

ACTIVITY -- -- TEXT PAGE 176 ~~~~~~~~~ Portfolio Assessments
with Video Vignette

See the CD-ROM Section of the Instructor's Manual.

ENDING EXERCISES -- -- CHAPTER 6

A. MEMORIZATION and COMPREHENSION EXERCISES
Low-Level Thought Activities -- PAGE 176

1. Because 1 cubic centimeter is the volume of 1 gram of mass and
   the capacity of 1 milliliter, the following would be true for 1 liter:

Capacity	Mass	Volume
1 liter =	1 kg or 1000 g	1 cu. meter or 1 m

2. Nonstandard units differ among peoples. Examples include
   "stepping off," hands-length, outstretched arms. Standard units
   do not differ. Examples include liters, quarts, miles, inches, tons,
   pounds, etc.
3. Examples of direct and indirect comparison are found
   throughout this chapter, beginning on page 154.
4. Answers will vary, depending on state chosen.

B. APPLICATION and ANALYSIS EXERCISES
Middle-Level Thought Activities -- PAGE 177

1. Answers will vary.
2. See text page 173.
3. Answers will vary, depending on the concepts chosen.

C. SYNTHESIS and EVALUATION EXERCISES
High-Level Thought Activities -- PAGE 177

1. This exercise requires the college students to develop a unit
   (series of lessons) on a concept of their choice. Continuity
   between lessons with review at the start of each new lesson is
   important and should be seen in the students' work. The
   answers will vary, depending on the grade level selected for this
   activity. More challenging lessons should be seen for upper
   grade children stressing decimal relationships and multi-step

strategies among the variables of money, metric measure, and numeration.

2.   Answers will vary depending upon the project or activities

3. } chosen.

4.

ACTIVITY ANSWERS -- -- CHAPTER 7

ACTIVITY -- -- TEXT PAGE 184 ~~~~~~~~~~ Sorting Projects

Activity answers will vary, depending on the classification scheme used in sorting. Examples are given in the activity on text page 164.

ACTIVITY -- -- TEXT PAGE 186 ~~~~~~~~~~ Spill the Beans

Activity answers will vary, depending on a child's understanding of the conservation of number.

Evaluation: If a child continues to count the entire set when the sum of the beans has not changed, it shows the child's lack of mathematical logic.

ACTIVITY -- -- TEXT PAGE 191 ~~~~~~~~~~ Finding Patterns in
                                              Our Lives

Activity answers will vary. Examples are given in the activity.

ACTIVITY -- -- TEXT PAGE 194 ~~~~~~~~~~ Assessment of
                                              Number Acquisition

The activity explains the different actions between a child who understands the meaning of number and a child who does not.

ACTIVITY -- -- TEXT PAGE 195 ~~~~~~~~~~ Portfolio Assessment

Answers will vary.
Among the materials that could be collected: beans, chips, pattern blocks, colored beads (jewels), number cards, tiles.

The interview protocol should follow the ideas in Chapter 4, particularly those on text page 108.
A checklist of characteristics could be a helpful rubric here.

Only suggestions for one series of activities are given here as a model: A child having difficulty with 1-1 correspondence may be focusing geometrically (size) rather than quantitatively (number amount). Begin with manipulatives that are similar in size (crayons and chalk); move on to manipulatives less similar in size (paper clips and books) -- but staying with small quantities, differing only by one or two. When these comparisons are easier, then increase the number of objects in each group. When you feel the child understands this now, then go to objects that are at a distance that cannot be brought into direct 1-1 comparison.

ACTIVITY -- -- TEXT PAGE 196 ~~~~~~~~~~ Developing More and
Less

Activity answers will vary. Examples are given in the activity.

ACTIVITY -- -- TEXT PAGE 198 ~~~~~~~~~~ Number Sequence on
a Calculator

Some calculators work differently. If students bring their calculators to class, the whole group can evaluate which types of calculators are the best for young children to use.

ENDING EXERCISES -- -- CHAPTER 7

A. MEMORIZATION and COMPREHENSION EXERCISES
Low-Level Thought Activities -- PAGE 199

1. Activities to help reversal problems:
   Provide tactile experiences, such as:
   a. Trace with fingers over sandpaper numerals or other textured material.
   b. With fingers, trace a numeral on someone's back while that person reproduces the same numeral on the chalkboard after "feeling" the first person's finger movements.
   c. Trace numerals in a small pan filled with salt and painted on the bottom with "glow-in-the-dark" paint so each numeral shines brightly as it is traced.
   Provide verbal feedback on the sequence needed for writing numerals.

For example:

To write the numeral, 4, the teacher says, "Start at the top of the line, come half way down, slide to the right, lift the pencil to the top of the line again, make a straight line down to the bottom of the line."

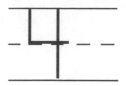

2. Some techniques to simulate manipulatives and help children develop an understanding of the operation of subtraction:
   a. Cut out flannel board pieces so the birds can actually leave the flannel board to simulate flying.
   b. Children can act out the pictures so the physical movements of leaving the scene (subtraction) can take place.
   c. Bring junk items from home and let the junk stand for the materials mentioned in the children's textbooks. The student can remove the items to simulate subtraction.

These are only a few ideas; the college students may think of many more.

B. APPLICATION and ANALYSIS EXERCISES
Middle-Level Thought Activities -- PAGE 199

1. Answers will vary, depending on the position taken by the teacher in the simulation. Justification of the person's position should be clearly seen by the wording the person chooses to explain his/her position to the mother-aide.

2. Answers will vary, depending on the textbook chosen.

3. The question is much the same as question 1 and could be handled in much the same way.

C. SYNTHESIS and EVALUATION EXERCISES
High-Level Thought Activities -- PAGE 199

1. The evaluation plan for testing if a child can count rationally should include some activities based on the concepts and tests of Piaget and Baratta-Lorton covered in this chapter.

2. Answers will vary. Students can use commercial catalogs to evaluate which manipulatives are worth buying and which ones could be handmade more economically and still be used effectively in the classroom.

3. Answers will vary, depending on the position taken by the student.

4. The question can used as an essay over the important points covered in the chapter. Each instructor may wish to set his/her own standards for the number of points and content to be covered in an acceptable essay.

<u>ACTIVITY--TEXT PAGE 204</u> ~~~~~~~~~~ Chinese Numeration
System

Students will probably be surprised to discover that a type of abacus
was used by the Greeks and Romans as well as the Chinese and
Japanese.
The abacus works on the principle of place-value notation;
consequently, relatively few beads are required to depict large
numbers.

<u>ACTIVITY--TEXT PAGE 207</u> ~~~~~~~~~~ Video Vignette

See the CD-ROM section of the Instructor's Manual.

<u>ACTIVITY -- TEXT PAGE 208</u> ~~~~~~~~~~ Base 4 Numeration
System

The following shows the multibase blocks and numerals in the base
four numeration systems to the third regrouping counting by units:

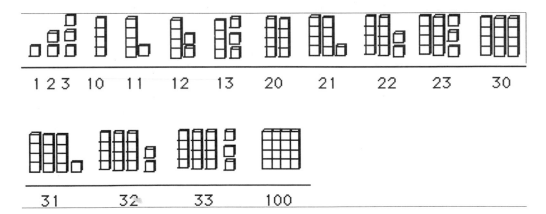

| 1 | 2 | 3 | 10 | 11 | 12 | 13 | 20 | 21 | 22 | 23 | 30 |

| 31 | 32 | 33 | 100 |

<u>ACTIVITY--TEXT PAGE 208</u> ~~~~~~~~~~ Numbers on the Wall

It was the discovery of zero that converted the Hindu-Arabic
notation into a place value system.
Answers will vary.

<u>ACTIVITY -- TEXT PAGE 209</u> ~~~~~~~~~ Let's Form the Numbers

Directions for using this activity with children are explained within
the activity itself. No answers are required here.

ACTIVITY -- TEXT PAGE 210 ~~~~~~~~~~ Place Value Strips--An
Aid to Mental Computation

Directions for using this activity with children are explained within
the activity itself. No answers are required here.

ACTIVITY -- TEXT PAGE 210 ~~~~~~~~~~ Equal Names

Directions for using this activity with children are explained within
the activity itself. No answers are required here.

ACTIVITY -- TEXT PAGE 211 ~~~~~~~~~~ Using Calculators with
the Expanded Form

The activity below shows all the combinations possible:

Enter in the Calculator:	Read-out on the Calculator:
3000 + 40 + 6 =	3046
6 + 3000 + 40 =	3046
40 + 6 + 3000 =	3046
3000 + 6 + 40 =	3046
40 + 3000 + 6 =	3046
6 + 40 + 3000 =	3046

ACTIVITY -- TEXT PAGE 212 ~~~~~~~~~~ Place Value Bingo

Directions for using this activity with children are explained within
the activity itself. No answers are required here.

ACTIVITY--TEXT PAGE 213 ~~~~~~~~~~ Video Vignette

See the CD-ROM section of the Instructor's Manual.

ACTIVITY -- TEXT PAGE 213 ~~~~~~~~~~ Chip Trading

The directions and answers are explained within the activity itself.

Note: The color position is not significant as long as children
understand that the color to the left represents larger place value
numbers.

ACTIVITY -- TEXT PAGE 214 ~~~~~~~~~~ Handfuls

Directions for using this activity with children are explained within
the activity itself.
Answers will vary.

ACTIVITY -- TEXT PAGE 214 ~~~~~~~~~~ Beat the Sand!

Directions for using this activity with children are explained within the activity itself.

ACTIVITY -- TEXT PAGE 215 ~~~~~~~~~~ Odometer Mathematics

Directions for using this activity with children are explained within the activity itself. No answers are required here.

ACTIVITY -- TEXT PAGE 216 ~~~~~~~~~~ Count on Five--Game 1
Count on Five--Game 2

Examples are given within each of the activities. No answers are required here.

ACTIVITY -- TEXT PAGE 216 ~~~~~~~~~~ Problem Solving
Through Patterns in Digit Hunt

Directions for playing the game are given within the activity.

ACTIVITY -- TEXT PAGE 216 ~~~~~~~~~~ Hundreds Chart Fun

Directions for using this activity with children are explained within the activity itself. No answers are required here.

ACTIVITY -- TEXT PAGE 217 ~~~~~~~~~~ Yup'ik Mathematics

Answers will vary.

ACTIVITY -- TEXT PAGE 218 ~~~~~~~~~~ Number Sense from
the Russian Perspective

Answers will vary.

ACTIVITY -- TEXT PAGE 218 ~~~~~~~~~~ Think about 1/2

Answers will vary.

ACTIVITIES -- TEXT PAGE 219 ~~~~~~~~~~ Number Sense and
Mental Computation
Think about 32.
The Answer is 5.
Make a Number.
High-Middle-Low

Directions are provided within the activities. Answers will vary.

ACTIVITY -- TEXT PAGE 220 ~~~~~~~~~~~ What Happens to the
                                                    Number if ... ?

26 + 38 =
- Sum increases by 2
- Sum increases by 1
- Sum remains the same

4 x 12 =
- Product increases by 17
- Product decreases by 15
- Product increases by 17
- Product decreases by 12

ACTIVITY -- TEXT PAGE 220 ~~~~~~~~~~ What's a Million Like?

Answers will vary. (See also the Activity on text page 221.)
It would take 100 minutes, or an hour and 40 minutes, to spend a
thousand dollars at the rate of $10 a minute.
A million dollars at that rate would be 100,000 minutes or a little
over 69 days.
A billion dollars at that rate would be 100,000,000 minutes or nearly
200 years.

ACTIVITY -- TEXT PAGE 221 ~~~~~~~~~~ Interpreting Large
                                                   Numbers

1. The largest number in the world:
   Prove to children that there is no largest number by giving the
   next number to any number they suggest. After several
   examples, ask them what it proves.

   The smallest number in the world:
   Some teachers of young children accept zero or one when it is
   suggested as a counting system. By middle school, students will
   learn about the negative integers and will be able to generalize
   from "argument" about the largest number.
2. The same procedure (seen in step 1) can be used when writing
   numbers.
3. Show the picture on text page 209 to generalize the pattern by:

       hundred   ten   one

4. There is no number called a "zillion". It is natural for humans to invent a vocabulary word that stands for "more numbers than the mind can imagine". Since "z" is at the end of the alphabet, to use the word "zillion" means the number is way out there in the system (infinity) of numbers.

5. It might be helpful to set some parameters, e.g., counting at the rate of 1 number per second without stopping. Under those conditions, 60 numbers per minute x 60 minutes per hour x 24 hours per day (60 x 60 x 24) would be 86,400 numbers per day. 10 days would be 864,000; 11 days would be 950,400 numbers. So, to count to one million at the rate of 1 number per second would take 11+ days.

Set up a proportion, using the number of minutes/days found to count to a million, and project the number of days/months it would take to count to a billion and trillion:

$$\frac{time}{1000000} = \frac{x}{1000000000} = \frac{y}{1000000000000}$$

6. Some things in our environment where we could find a million? a billion?

a million	a billion
blades of grass in a yard	people (approximately 5 billion)
dollars in state lotteries	snowflakes in a storm
germs during flu season	United States deficit

7. How many pages would it take to make a million dots?
   Picture 100 dots in a half inch square.
   Regular size paper = 8 1/2" x 11"
   Paper would have 17 columns and 22 rows of 100 dots

$$\begin{array}{r} 17 \text{ columns} \\ \times\ 22 \text{ rows} \\ \hline \end{array}$$

   374 squares of 100 dots = 374000 dots on one page

   1000000 dots ÷ 374000 dots = 26.737968 pages
   Answer: 26 and 3/4 pages

8. Just looking at the numbers in step 6 shows how hard it is for a person's eyes to focus on a long number, and it illustrates how much space such numbers take up on a printed line. People want to read newspapers quickly and easily. Publishers want to print as many stories as possible in the space that they have.

9. Who was living a million minutes ago?

$$
\begin{array}{r}
60 \\
\times\ 24 \\
\hline
1440 \\
\times 365 \\
\hline
525{,}600 \\
\times\qquad 2 \\
\hline
1{,}051{,}200
\end{array}
$$

   60   minutes in one hour
x 24 hours in a day
1440 minutes in one day
x365 days in one year
525,600 minutes in one year
x   2 to find how many minutes in two years
1,051,200 is over a million minutes in two years

Let's find which month is closest to the million mark:

$525{,}600 \div 12 = 43800$ minutes per month

For 10 months:
$$
\begin{array}{r}
43800 \\
\times\ 10 \\
\hline
438{,}000 \\
+\ 525{,}600 \\
\hline
963{,}600
\end{array}
$$
first year

For 11 months:
$$
\begin{array}{r}
43800 \\
\times\ 11 \\
\hline
481{,}800 \\
+\ 525{,}600 \\
\hline
1{,}007{,}400
\end{array}
$$
first year

1 year 10 months = slightly under a million minutes
1 year 11 months = slightly over a million minutes

Answer: Any one living 1 year and 11 months ago has lived slightly over a million minutes. Because seconds are smaller units than minutes, a person who has lived a million minutes or more has also lived more than a million seconds.

ACTIVITY -- TEXT PAGE 222 ~~~~~~~~~~ Rounding Large
                                                     Numbers

Directions for this activity are given in the activity.

ACTIVITY -- TEXT PAGE 223 ~~~~~~~~~~ Reading Decimal
                                                     Numbers

The first and fourth examples should be the easiest to understand when hearing the number read aloud by others.

ACTIVITY -- TEXT PAGE 223 ~~~~~~~~~~ Cover Up Game and
                                                    Add Some More

The examples are self-explanatory as they appear on text pages 223 and 224.

ACTIVITY -- TEXT PAGE 224 ~~~~~~~~~~ Different Ways to
                                       Represent Decimals

1.   0.4   0.7   0.45   0.758
     four-tenths   seven-tenths   forty-five   seven hundred
                                   hundredths   fifty-eight
                                                 thousandths

Step 2 and Step 3:
       These steps should be done with the actual concrete
       manipulatives, but they are seen here as step 4, the pictorial
       level. Steps 5 and 6 are also shown in the chart which follows
       on the next page.

ACTIVITY -- TEXT PAGE 226 ~~~~~~~~~~ Portfolio Assessments

Answers will vary but among the comments the following should
be anticipated:
The first child is demonstrating a variety of ways that s/he knows
for making 6. The use of parentheses, subtraction, and even a
multiplication indicate some interesting awarenesses. It should
also be noted that all of the facts are "basic."
The second child is demonstrating a variety of ways of expressing
the number 434 in place value expansions. Some of the
combinations are quite sophisticated.
The third child has labeled groups whose written value would
equal the target number. However, the blocks (with the exception
of the units) are not appropriately drawn for representing base nine.

There should be 3 rubrics, one for each student. The rubrics should
include the aspects noted above plus others that the college students
has appropriately identified.

The most important thing, perhaps, that you would like to know
about each of these children is the grade level, and place value/
numeration activities prior to these samples of their work.
The first student might be introduced to the use of larger numbers
... i.e., 20-14; 30-24; (20 + 10) - 24.
There are many directions that next steps for the second child could
take. No doubt the college students will have a wide variety of
appropriate suggestions.
The third child would probably benefit from returning to the
concrete multi-base blocks, perhaps playing "Build a Cube" in base

nine. Proportional activities at this point would be more appropriate than non-proportional (i.e., chip trading).

ENDING EXERCISES -- -- CHAPTER 7

A. MEMORIZATION and COMPREHENSION EXERCISES
Low-Level Thought Activities -- PAGE 227

1. The student is confusing the number-name with its written standardized form.
2. Typically, when using base 10 blocks for decimals, the thousands cube is the ones unit; the flat represents tenths; the long represents hundredths; and the single (small) cube represents thousandths. Thus, 0.08 would consist of 8 longs; 0.80 would be represented by 8 flats. Using graph paper, a ten by ten grid would be the simplest model. 0.08 would be shown by 8 of the small squares colored; 0.80 would be shown by 80 of the small squares (8 rows of 10 squares, e.g.) colored.
3. Base 2

1	10	11	100	101	110
111	1000	1001	1010	1011	1100
1101	1110	1111	10000	10001	10010
10011	10100	10101	10110	10111	11000
11001	11010	11011	11100	11101	11110

Base 5

1	2	3	4	10	11
12	13	14	20	21	22
23	24	30	31	32	33
34	40	41	42	43	44
100	101	102	103	104	110

Base 8

1	2	3	4	5	6
7	10	11	12	13	14
15	16	17	20	21	22
23	24	25	26	27	30
31	32	33	34	35	36

The patterns that students will vary.

The first four place value configurations should be based on the model shown in Figure 8.4 on page 209 of the text. Similarities that might be noted include the repetition of the unit, long, flat in each period of the given system; in each base, there is one less of any given block than the base itself.

B. APPLICATION and ANALYSIS EXERCISES
Middle-Level Thought Activities -- PAGE 227

1. The number 214 does NOT exist in base three because all sets are regrouped at three and there is no need for any numeral greater than two to be used.

   In base five, the number 214 could be represented by multi-base blocks like the following:

   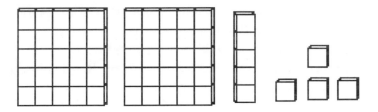

   In base nine, the number 214 could be represented by multi-base blocks like the following:

   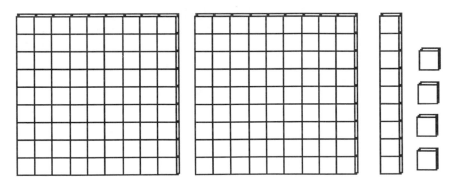

   Similarly, in base fifteen, the number 214 could be represented by multi-base blocks like the above -- 2 flats of 15, a long of 15 and 4 singles.

2. The numbers in B1 would look like this on the chip trading mat:

Green	Red	Blue
⊛ ⊛	⊛	⊛ ⊛ ⊛ ⊛

214 base five
214 base nine
214 base fifteen

Look all the
same on the
chip trading mat

In working with base two numbers, more color columns need to be added for each additional place value.

3. Answers will vary depending upon the ideas found in the current journals.

C. SYNTHESIS and EVALUATION EXERCISES
High-Level Thought Activities -- PAGE 228

1. The lesson plans will vary, depending on the concept chosen from the NCTM Standards.
2. The following number line goes to the number 20 in the first regrouping in base seven.

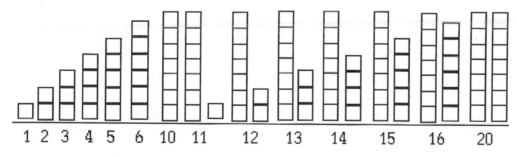

3. Answers will vary, depending on the symbols chosen for the numerals in the student's individual numeration system.
4. Answers will vary.
5. Answers will vary.

ACTIVITY ANSWERS -- -- CHAPTER 9

<u>ACTIVITY -- TEXT PAGE 246</u> ~~~~~~~~~ Bridging to 10

Examples to use with children are given in the activity on text page 246.

<u>ACTIVITY -- TEXT PAGE 246</u> ~~~~~~~~~ Video Vignette

See the CD-ROM section of the instructor's manual.

<u>ACTIVITY -- TEXT PAGE 247</u> ~~~~~~~~~ Using the Calculator
                                        with Basic Facts

2. The calculator stores the first number entered and adds it to each succeeding number that is entered into the calculator. It is important to push the equal sign after each number.
3. Or, you can do this with partners. The child with the calculator says the sum aloud; the partner writes it down on a slate board then the "=" sign is pushed and the answer checked.

<u>ACTIVITY -- TEXT PAGE 247</u> ~~~~~~~~~ Real-World Math --
                                Exploring Basic Operations of Subtraction

1. $8 + p = 17$ or $17 - 8 = p$
2. $15 - 9 = c$
3. $15 - c = 9$ or $9 + n = 15$

<u>ACTIVITY -- TEXT PAGE 250</u> ~~~~~~~~~ Subtract the Whole/
                                        Almost the Whole

The activity is explained on text page 250.

<u>ACTIVITY -- TEXT PAGE 250</u> ~~~~~~~~~ Chinese Multiplication
                                        Table

5. Answers will vary.

<u>ACTIVITY -- TEXT PAGE 251</u> ~~~~~~~~~ Multiplication as
                                        Repeated Addition

The first tasks are self-explanatory.

The related multiplication equation for the last six tasks are:
1. 4×3

2. 5 x 8
3. 3 x 1
4. 4 x 6
5. (4 x 4) + (2 x 23)
6. 3 x 7

If your calculator has a "Constant" key, the answer to:
        8 + === will be be 32.

ACTIVITY -- TEXT PAGE 253 ~~~~~~~~~ Finding Multiples

Multiples of 5

1. 10, 15, 20, 25, 30, 35, 40, 45, 50, 55, 60, 65, 70, 75, 80, 85, 90, 95, 100
2. 0 and 5
3. Yes, if the chart is extended, the tens place value continues in the
   same pattern.
4. $25 = 2 + 5 = 7$
   $35 = 3 + 5 = 8$
   $45 = 4 + 5 = 9$
   $55 = 5 + 5 = 10$
   $65 = 6 + 5 = 11$
        etc.

5. Because the numbers in the ones place value alternate between 5
   and 0, they are easy to remember and young children seem to
   learn them more easily than other combinations.

Multiples of 9
Steps 1 through 4 are answered within the activity.

Multiples of 3
1. Answered in step 3 below
2. Answered in step 3 below
3.   3   6   9
       12   15   18
       21   24   27
4. The digits of the two-digit numbers when added together equal
   the number at the end of each column (as seen in step 3 above.)
5.   odd   even   odd
        even   odd   even
        odd   even   odd
   The multiples of 3 have an alternating odd/even pattern.
6. Answers will vary.

ENDING EXERCISES -- -- CHAPTER 9

A. MEMORIZATION and COMPREHENSION EXERCISES
Low-Level Thought Activities -- PAGE 263

1. Linking cubes or unifix cubes, or chips, are examples of other concrete materials that could be used to show the commutative and associative properties. If a student was to demonstrate the commutative property using 2 + 3 = 3 + 2, a group of 2 red cubes and a group of 3 green cubes could be joined in either order to create a set of 5 cubes. Similarly for the chips, which might be placed in small cups to clearly delineate the sets of 2 and 3. A similar approach could be taken for the associative property, showing, for example, that (2 + 3) + 4 = 2 + (3 + 4).

2. Partitive division means you have the whole and are trying to find out how many would go in each of a specified number of groups. Examples similar to those on text page 239 are appropriate. Measurement division means you have the whole and are trying to find out how many groups would get a specified number. Examples similar to those on text page 238 are appropriate.

3. Answers will vary but should include the idea that contradictions arise within our understanding of the inverse relationship between multiplication and division.

B. APPLICATION and ANALYSIS EXERCISES
Middle-Level Thought Activities -- PAGE 263

All the answers in this section will vary, depending on the examples and concepts chosen by the student.

C. SYNTHESIS and EVALUATION EXERCISES
High-Level Thought Activities -- PAGE 263

1. The lesson plans will vary, depending on the concept chosen from the NCTM Standards.

2. Assessment of the child's work with the multiplication table follows the analytic questions asked in steps a through e:
   a. The child gets the correct answer along the top row but is not consistent when doing the same basic facts down the column. Because there are other problems related to the chart form of the worksheet, it could be the format that is the problem rather than a misconception about zero.
   b. The child begins to have problems when dealing with factors of three or more. The child shows a knowledge of

multiplication of sets in the tally marks drawn for 3 x 3 and continuing down the column of factors of three, modeling the correct meaning of multiplication. However, when the same basic facts are to be worked going across the rows, the tally marks indicate the student is simply "adding 3" to the preceding number.

c. The child begins to "add three" to each number after 3 x 4. The "adding 3" is seen again beginning with 4 x 4.

d. The child begins to "add three" from one product to the next without regard to the multiplier or once the student is beyond "x3."

e. The child knows the identity element (multiplication by 1's), 2's, and 5's. The 5's are correct only when done going across the chart instead of down the columns.

NOTE: The child may be a field dependent learner asked to do the detailed work of filling in the chart. The eye movements required to fill in each square after looking at the top and side number may be overwhelming to the student because the work deteriorates as the squares become farther away from the top and side factors.

3. The plan of remediation will vary, depending on each student's view of the problem. The student should notice the following error patterns:

a. The student answers the basic facts correctly until the last two rows when the correct answers fall off dramatically.

b. The student has trouble with addition and subtraction facts with 9 and knows that some help is needed to figure them out. The tally marks are very small but seem to be effective in arriving at the correct answer, and evidence that some pictorial manipulations are still needed.

c. The last four numbers are consecutive 4, 5, 6, 7 and seem to be written in a hurry without really looking at the number combination to be added.

d. This seems to be the kind of child who needs to have fewer problems given at a time, and may be considered a field independent learner who does not do well when confronted with a large number of problems to do at a time. The child may be more successful if two rows are given at a time. In more dire circumstances, a child may be given a folder with a window cut out just the size of one problem. As the problem is answered, the child moves the window in the folder to the next problem.

4. Answers will vary, depending on the position taken by the student.

ACTIVITY ANSWERS -- -- CHAPTER 10

<u>ACTIVITY -- TEXT PAGE 273</u> ~~~~~~~~~~~ Algorithms from Other Cultures

The activity is self-explanatory on text page 273.

<u>ACTIVITY -- TEXT PAGE 275</u> ~~~~~~~~~~~ Teaching Addition with Regrouping

The activity is self-explanatory on text page 275.

<u>ACTIVITY -- TEXT PAGE 276</u> ~~~~~~~~~~~ Video Vignette

See the CD-ROM section of this instructor's manual.

<u>ACTIVITY -- TEXT PAGE 276</u> ~~~~~~~~~~~ Addition Practice

1)

876	+	**495**	=	1371
+		+		+
709	+	**632**	=	1341
=		=		=
1585	+	**1127**	+	**2712**

2)

892	+	**400**	=	1292
+		+		+
641	+	**357**	=	998
=		=		=
1533	+	**757**	=	**2290**

ACTIVITY -- TEXT PAGE 276 ~~~~~~~~~~ Double Trouble

The activity is self-explanatory on text page 276.

ACTIVITY -- TEXT PAGE 277 ~~~~~~~~~~ Spend Exactly $3.55

Chp	Mlk	Coco	App	Hdo	Hmb	Cbar	Orng	Ban	Pop	IceC	Ckie
2			1					2		1	
2			1	1		1				1	
		1	1	1		1	1				
					1				2		1
	1			1	1						
	2				1					1	
1		1			1						1
1	3		1								
		4						1			
1			2		1		1				
				2		1			1		
		1			2						

(No one said these had to be healthy combinations!) No doubt students will find other combinations as well, and yes, there are more than 10 combinations.

ACTIVITY -- TEXT PAGE 277 ~~~~~~~~~~ Teaching Take-Away
Subtraction with Regrouping

The activity is self-explanatory as it appears on text pages 277- 278.

ACTIVITY -- TEXT PAGE 278 ~~~~~~~~~~ Teaching Comparison
Subtraction with Regrouping

The activity is self-explanatory as it appears on text page 278.

ACTIVITY -- TEXT PAGE 279 ~~~~~~~~~~ Teaching Missing
Addend for Subtraction with Regrouping

The circled amount below shows what is needed to bring the scale into balance.

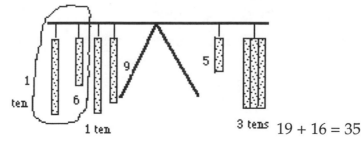

$19 + 16 = 35$

ACTIVITY -- TEXT PAGE 280 ~~~~~~~~~~ Modeling Multiplication

The answer is self-explanatory as it appears in the activity on text pages 280-281.

ACTIVITY -- TEXT PAGE 282 ~~~~~~~~~~ Prove It

An example is given within the activity on text page 282.

ACTIVITY -- TEXT PAGE 282 ~~~~~~~~~~ Copy Method

The answer is self-explanatory as it appears in the activity on text pages 282-83.

ACTIVITY -- TEXT PAGE 283 ~~~~~~~~~~ Multiplication

An example is given within the activity on text page 283.

ACTIVITY -- TEXT PAGE 284 ~~~~~~~~~~ Video Vignette

See the CD-ROM section of this instructor's manual.

ACTIVITY -- TEXT PAGE 286 ~~~~~~~~~~ Division Patterns with the Calculator

The correct pathways appear below:

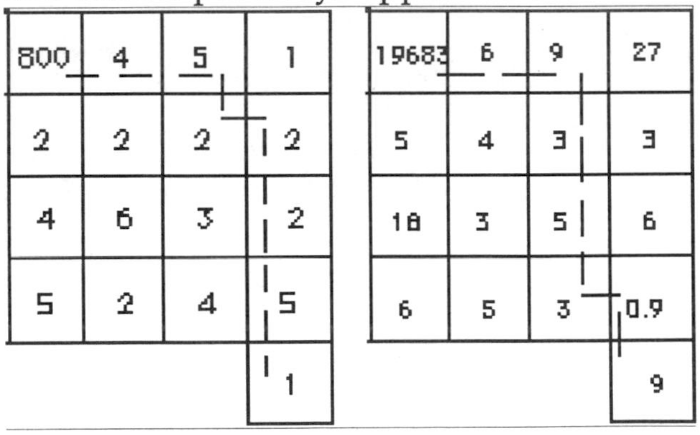

800	4	5	1
2	2	2	2
4	6	3	2
5	2	4	5
			1

19683	6	9	27
5	4	3	3
18	3	5	6
6	5	3	0.9
			9

ACTIVITY -- TEXT PAGE 287 ~~~~~~~~~~ Leftovers

Directions are self-explanatory.

ACTIVITY -- TEXT PAGE 288 ~~~~~~~~~~ Use Those Fours!

Sample solutions are given here. Students are encouraged to find as many as they can.

$0 = (4+4) \times (4 - 4)$ $1 = 4 + (4 / 4) - 4$
$2 = (4 / 4) + (4 / 4)$ $3 = (4+4+4) / 4$
$4 = 4 \times (4 - 4) + 4$ $5 = [(4 \times 4) + 4] / 4$
$6 = [(4 + 4) / 4] + 4$ $7 = (4 + 4) - (4 / 4)$
$8 = (4 \times 4) - (4 + 4)$ $9 = 4 + (4 / 4) + 4$
$10 = [(44 - 4)] / 4$

ACTIVITY -- TEXT PAGE 288 ~~~~~~~~~~ Fill It Up

Directions are self-explanatory.

ACTIVITY -- TEXT PAGE 289 ~~~~~~~~~~ "I Have ..."

Directions are self-explanatory.
Some suggestions for students who want to create their own sets:
1. Make a list of the range of numbers that will be used as the solution. Then create problems for each ... you want to be sure that each solution is used only once.
2. Have extras in your set. Some can be "distractors" that will keep a distractible student attentive ... with 2 cards, only one of which is used in the round. A teacher who knows his/her students can plant these distractor cards appropriately.
3. Encourage students to work to continuously improve on their class "time" needed to complete the set.
4. Sets can be made up for many topics ... geometry, probability, single operations, multi-step problems.

ACTIVITY -- TEXT PAGE 290 ~~~~~~~~~~ Missing Numbers

Implied in the directions is that each of the digits, 5 through 9, is placed once and only once in the placeholders given.

LARGEST ANSWER
$875 \times 96 = 84{,}000$ $986 + 75 = 1061$ $987 - 56 = 931$

$9876 / 5 = 1975.2$

SMALLEST ANSWER
$589 \times 76 = 39{,}463$ $567 + 89 = 656$ $567 - 98 = 469$

$5678 / 9 = 630.8$

Answers will vary.

ACTIVITY -- TEXT PAGE 290 ~~~~~~~~~~ Use Your Head And Let's
Compute!

Directions are self-explanatory.

ACTIVITY -- TEXT PAGE 291 ~~~~~~~~~~ Estimation Detectives
Front-End Estimation!

Directions are self-explanatory.

ACTIVITY -- TEXT PAGE 291 ~~~~~~~~~~ Are We Compatible?

"Friendly numbers" provide easy combinations ... e.g., tens, fives,
when adding.

ACTIVITY -- TEXT PAGE 292 ~~~~~~~~~~ Targeting Products

Directions are self-explanatory.

ENDING EXERCISES -- -- CHAPTER 10

A. MEMORIZATION and COMPREHENSION EXERCISES
Low-Level Thought Activities -- PAGE 298

1. The two types of division are partitive (fair sharing) and
   measurement (successive subtraction) division. See Chapter 9
   for further explanations. Examples of each will vary, depending
   on student response. However, the examples should be like
   those presented on text page 285.
2. Estimation helps the student know if the answer is a reasonable
   one. Rounding to the nearest ten, hundred, thousand, etc. helps
   students do the estimation quickly by using the place value
   structure of the number system when dealing with large
   numbers.
3. The answers should focus on the idea that long tedious
   calculations are not realistic to the experiences in the real work
   place where adults reach for a calculator and use estimation to
   check the reasonableness of the answers. The students should
   state that this is a recommendation made by the NCTM
   curriculum standards (Commission on Standards for School
   Mathematics, 1989). More information is found on text pages
   301 and 302.

B. APPLICATION and ANALYSIS EXERCISES
    Middle-Level Thought Activities -- PAGE 298

1. Answers will vary, depending on the manipulative material chosen.
2. The copy method of division is presented below:

$$\overline{21 \mid 672}$$

$$\overline{21 \mid 678}$$

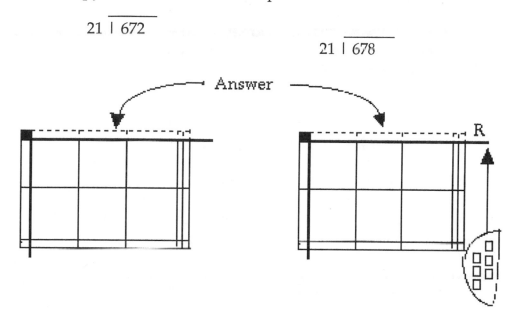

3. The algorithm created by the bright fourth grader will work with any multi-digit problem. It works because it is based on the place value concept of ones, tens, hundreds, etc. The student knew that any number in the dividend can be divided by any number in the divisor whether the divisor is presented in its compact notation (ex = 23) or its expanded notation (ex = 20 + 3). The important thing is to remember to use each part of the expanded divisor, alternating back and forth after each subtraction in the dividend.

C. SYNTHESIS and EVALUATION EXERCISES
    High-Level Thought Activities -- PAGE 298

1. Answers will vary, depending on the algorithm process chosen.
2. Answers will vary, depending on the concept chosen.
3. The question can be used as an essay stressing the important points covered in the chapter. Each instructor may wish to set his/her own standards for the number of points and content to be covered in an acceptable essay.

ACTIVITY -- TEXT PAGE 299 ~~~~~~~~~ Portfolio Assessments

An assessment of each child's worksheet follows:

With Subtraction:

a. Error Pattern Analysis
1) The child always regroups whether it is needed or not. The regrouping at the left is shown as zero because there is nothing remaining to the left to be regrouped and this equates as a "zero" in this child's logic.
2) The child always makes the regrouped number one less when switching to the next column to the right.
3) The child always subtracts the largest numeral from the smallest no matter what its position as the minuend or subtrahend.
4) The child knows the basic number facts well; they do NOT seem to be a factor in the child's misconceptions.

b. Evaluation of Thought Processing
Four problems are too small a number to assess a student's total processing style. Teachers need to be looking for this factor as one piece in the puzzle of diagnosing problems. If the college student can see the rationale for each processing style and state it clearly, credit should be given. For example:
1) A Field Dependent Learner
The child may be a field dependent learner, preferring simultaneous thought processing, who is trying to make sense out of an algorithm that requires action on the parts (ones, tens, hundreds, thousands, etc.) when it is not natural for the child to look for such minute detail. The child renames the whole number in the minuend before attempting to subtract -- a tendency seen in simultaneous learners. This strategy would have worked well if the child had not tried to flip to the detail subtraction using a field independent (successive processing) approach at an inappropriate time.
2) A Field Independent Learner
The child may be a field independent learner, preferring successive thought processing, who sees each part as it it were a separate problem without ever considering the number as a whole. It's as if three problems (in this case of hundreds) were squeezed on the page close together, and the child never thinks of the problem as one large number. This can be discerned by the teacher if he/she asks the child to state the problem orally. A successive learner would start reading each column as if it were a simple basic fact. For example, in the first problem the child would say, "five take away four," instead of eight hundred thirty four with two hundred five taken away.

c. Sequential Development
   The concrete, pictorial, and symbolic models will vary, depending upon the activities chosen by the student, but the sequential progression from the concrete to the symbolic should be seen if credit is to be given for this part of the remedial plan.

d. Rubric
   Since these are not open-ended questions, students may find it easier to develop a rubric in more of a checklist format, listing the facets or elements of mathematics needed to successfully perform the given operation. The various rating categories might be: competent (complete understanding - 5), needs improvement (partial understanding - 3), not yet (no answer, no understanding - 0). Credit should be given for this part if the college student identifies the essential components of the task, with adequate descriptors.

With Multiplication:

a. Error Pattern Analysis
   1) The child knows that in a multi-digit multiplication problem, there is addition involved; the child just does not know which part is to be added and which part is to be multiplied.
   2) The child starts each example correctly by multiplying the ones column, obtaining the correct answer, but the child writes the "tens" place value in the "ones" place value and regroups the "ones" place value over to the "tens" column.
   3) The child then adds all numerals in the tens column.
   4) The same procedure is followed as in step 2 and step 3 (above) when the child handles the original top factor by the bottom factor in the tens column.
   5) The child then finishes the total problem by multiplying the two partial products instead of adding them as the traditional algorithm requires.

b. Evaluation of Thought Processing
   The same philosophy for giving credit should be followed as stated in the subtraction problems above.

c. Sequential Development
   The same philosophy for giving credit should be followed as stated in the subtraction problems above.

d. Rubric
   The same philosophy for giving credit should be followed as stated in the subtraction problems above.

The following Cuisenaire rods represent one-third:

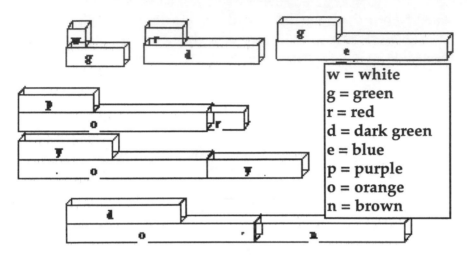

| w = white |
| g = green |
| r = red |
| d = dark green |
| e = blue |
| p = purple |
| o = orange |
| n = brown |

One can prove that the top rod is exactly one-third of the basic
building unit (the bottom rod) by putting two more rods on the
top, thereby showing that the first rod was really one-third of the
basic unit as demonstrated below:

| white | | red |
| green | | dark green |

The Cuisenaire rods below represent two-thirds:

| red |
| green |
| purple |
| dark green |
| blue |

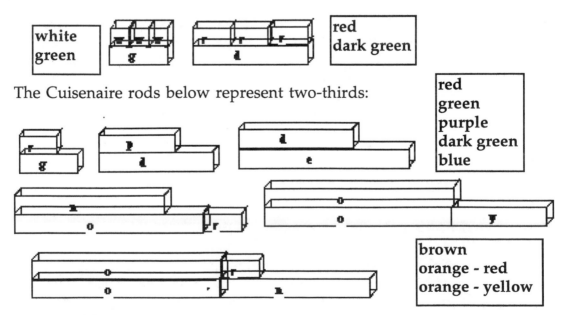

| brown |
| orange - red |
| orange - yellow |

The proof that the top rod in each combination is exactly two-thirds
of the basic unit (bottom rod) can be proven using the same
procedure as outlined in step 2 above.

ACTIVITY -- TEXT PAGE 307 ~~~~~~~~~ Name the Fraction -
Find the Whole
Edible Fractions!

Directions for these activities are contained within the text, page 307.

ACTIVITY -- TEXT PAGE 308 ~~~~~~~~~ Origins of Fractions
What's the Part?

Directions for these activities are contained within the text, page 308.

ACTIVITY -- TEXT PAGE 309 ~~~~~~~~~ Making a Rectangular
Fraction Kit
Partitioning Regions

The directions are contained within the activities and require no explanation here.

ACTIVITY -- TEXT PAGE 310 ~~~~~~~~~ Equivalent Fractions:
Fraction Strip Chart

The use of the fraction strip chart is self-explanatory on text pages 309 and 310. The chart itself appears on text page 309 as Figure 11.7.

ACTIVITY -- TEXT PAGE 310 ~~~~~~~~~ Rolling Equivalents
Fraction War
Fractions on the Geoboard

The directions are contained within the activities and require no explanation here.

ACTIVITY -- TEXT PAGE 311 ~~~~~~~~~ Video Vignette

See the CD-ROM section of the instructor's manual.

ACTIVITY -- TEXT PAGE 312 ~~~~~~~~~ Equivalent Fractions:
Multiple Bars

The use of the multiple bars is self-explanatory on text page 312. The chart itself appear on text page 311 as Figure 11.8.

ACTIVITY -- TEXT PAGE 312 ~~~~~~~~~ Game 1 -- Cover Up

The directions for the game are contained within the activity itself.

ACTIVITY -- TEXT PAGE 313 ~~~~~~~~~~ Game 2 -- Uncover

The directions for the game are contained within the activity itself.

ACTIVITY -- TEXT PAGE 315 ~~~~~~~~~~ Showing Geoboard
Operations

Directions for the activity are contained within the activity itself.

ACTIVITY -- TEXT PAGE 316 ~~~~~~~~~~ Estimate and Order
Roll and Show

The directions are contained within the activities and require no explanation here.

ACTIVITY -- TEXT PAGE 317 ~~~~~~~~~~ Estimation with
Fractions

Problems with fractional portions:

$7/12 + 3/6$ = about 1 $4/10 + 11/10$ = about 1 1/2

$2/9 + 7/8$ = about 1 $9/20 + 4/5$ = about 1 1/2

$8/9 - 4/5$ = about 0 $10/9 - 1/12$ = about 1

Problems with whole numbers and fractions:

2 4/5 + 2 9/10 = about 6   3 1/9 + 8 8/10 = about 12

7 - 2 6/7 = about 4   4 8/12 - 7/9 = about 4

ACTIVITY -- TEXT PAGE 318 ~~~~~~~~~~ Multiplying Fractions--
Whole Number by a Fractional Number

The materials are modeled and explained within the activity itself on text page 318.

ACTIVITY -- TEXT PAGE 319 ~~~~~~~~~~ Multiplying Fractions--
Fractional Number by Fractional Number

The materials are modeled and explained within the activity itself on text page 319.

ACTIVITY -- TEXT PAGE 320 ~~~~~~~~~~ Understanding
                              Multiplication of Fractions

The materials are modeled and explained within the activity itself
on text page 320.

ACTIVITY -- TEXT PAGE 320 ~~~~~~~~~~ Division of Fractional
                    Numbers-- Whole Number by a Fraction

The materials are modeled and explained within the activity itself
on text pages 320 and 321.

ACTIVITY -- TEXT PAGE 321 ~~~~~~~~~~ Using the Common
                              Denominator Method

The materials are modeled and explained within the activity itself
on text pages 321 and 322.

ACTIVITY -- TEXT PAGE 322 ~~~~~~~~~~ Division of Fractional
                    Numbers--Fraction by a Fraction

The materials are modeled and explained within the activity itself
on text pages 322 and 323.

ACTIVITY -- TEXT PAGE 323 ~~~~~~~~~~ Rounding Mixed
                              Numbers in Division

The answers are given within the activity itself on text page 323.

ACTIVITY -- TEXT PAGE 323 ~~~~~~~~~~ Estimate and Sort

The materials are modeled and explained within the activity itself
on text page 323.

ACTIVITY -- TEXT PAGE 324 ~~~~~~~~~~ Fraction Cube Toss
                              Greatest Quotient

The directions are contained within the activities and require no
explanation here.

ACTIVITY -- TEXT PAGE 328 ~~~~~~~~~~ Terminating Decimals

On the next page is a base 10 number line like the one in Figure
    11.11 with one-fourth marked in the tenths, hundredths, and
    thousandths:

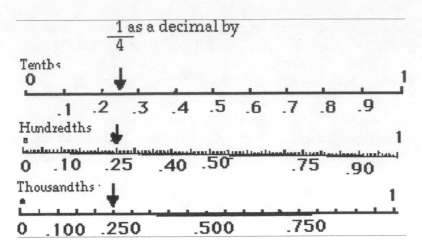

One discovers that there is no point marked on the number line in tenths for one-fourth, but there is a definite point on the hundredths and thousandths number line. That's one explanation for writing the decimal equivalent of one-fourth as .25 or 25 hundredths. One can read the decimal .25 as two-tenths and a half of the next tenth but it is rarely done.

Using the base 10 blocks, the same process can be seen. There is no way to divide the tenths into equal portions of fourths unless one goes to the hundredths or LONGS and regroups the remaining two-tenths as four sets of 5 hundredths. Again, the hundredths place is the point at which an equal portion of one-fourth can be seen. The process is illustrated on page 329 of the text.

If the procedures are applied to one-eighth, a definite point will not be seen on the number line until the thousandths place. With base 10 blocks, the whole number, 1, can be partitioned evenly only when using the smallest block, the thousandth block. Therefore, the same principle holds using different concrete manipulatives.

ACTIVITY -- TEXT PAGE 329 ~~~~~~~~~~ Non-terminating, Repeating Decimals

The activity is self-explanatory.

ACTIVITY -- TEXT PAGE 330 ~~~~~~~~~~ Division of Common Fractions into Decimals

1. The manipulations are set up and described as a part of step 3 so that the symbols, words and manipulatives can be seen together.

2. The question is asking---> "How many base 10 blocks are there in each set of 4 equal sets made from the whole number 2?"

   The question above represents partitive division. The question could be asked, using measurement division--"How many sets of 4 are there in the whole number two?" Either interpretation presents an efficient way to divide decimals for this example.

3. Using Partitive Division...
       With Symbols   In Words

```
        .50
    4 | 2.00            There are 5 tenths
       2 0              or 50 hundredths in each
                        set of 4 equal sets
```

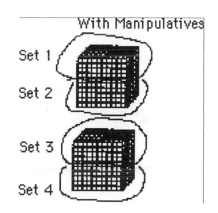

Using Measurement Division...
With Symbols   In Words

```
        .50
    4 | 2.00           There are 5 sets of 4
       2 0             in the tenths with no
                       further regrouping
                       needed in the whole
                       number 2.
```

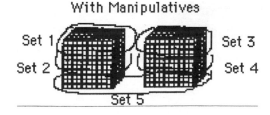

4. Doing the same thing with 1/8

The question is asking--> "How many sets of 8 are there in the whole number 1?"

NOTE TO INSTRUCTOR
The question above represents the most efficient way to divide the set; it is measurement division. The question could be asked, using partitive division-- "How many base 10 blocks are there in each set of 8 equal sets made from the whole number 1?" However, that question would necessitate dividing the base 10 block into 8 sets of 125, taking considerably more time and more manipulations. Students should opt for the most efficient way to divide decimals using either interpretation of division when appropriate to the model. That is the philosophy followed in the decimal activities found in Chapter 11.

With Symbols	In Words
.125	First division is in tenths. Only one set of 8 can
8 | 1.00	be made in the tenths, leaving 2 tenths to be re-
8	grouped as 20 hundredths. Two sets of 8 can be
20	made in the hundredths, leaving 4 hundredths
16	to be regrouped as 40 thousandths. Five sets of 8
40	can be made in the thousandths with no more
40	blocks to be regrouped.
0	

With Manipulations

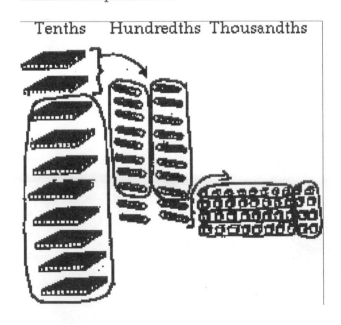

ACTIVITY -- TEXT PAGE 331 ~~~~~~~~~~~ Ladybug Round Off

The activity is self-explanatory.

ACTIVITY -- TEXT PAGE 332 ~~~~~~~~~~ Problem Solving with
                                    Decimals

1. If 3 bananas weigh 1 pound, then the cost of one banana (on average) would be $.23.
2. 3 1/2 lbs. will cost $5.22 (rounded to the next cent)
3. Each of the three miles is divided into eighths:

$$\text{first } \frac{1}{8} \text{ mile} = \$1.10$$

$$\frac{7}{8} + \frac{8}{8} + \frac{8}{8} + \frac{8}{8} = \frac{23}{8} \text{ so } 23 \times \$.35 = \underline{\$8.05}$$

$$\text{Total Cost} \qquad \$9.15$$

4. & 5. Answers will vary.

ACTIVITY -- TEXT PAGE 333 ~~~~~~~~~~~ Give Away

The activity is self-explanatory.

ACTIVITY -- TEXT PAGE 334 ~~~~~~~~~~ Rounding with Decimals

The remaining 4 examples should be filled in the chart as follows:

Problem	Mental Rounding	Estimated Answer	Actual Answer
11.34 - 0.895	Think: 11-1	About 10	10.445
1.11 - 0.999	Think: 1-1	Less than 1	0.111
345.25-245.5	Think: 345-246	About 100	99.75
0.927 - 0.398	Think: .9 - .4	About .5	0.529

ACTIVITY -- TEXT PAGE 334 ~~~~~~~~~~ Observation of
                                   Multiplication with Base 10 Blocks

1. Step 1 is self-explanatory.

2. The rest of the chart (with the first three included) is:

		Number of Deci mal Places in	
Problem	Answer	Problem	Answer
2 X 0.05	0.10	2	2
0.05 X 2	0.10	2	2
0.2 X 0.05	0.010	3	3
0.05 X 0.2	0.010	3	3
0.02 X 0.05	0.0010	4	4
0.05 X 0.02	0.0010	4	4

3. The pattern shows that the number of decimal places in the answer increases at the same rate as the number of decimal places in the problem.

4. The generalized rule:
   The number of decimal places in the total problem will also be the number of decimal places in the answer.

ACTIVITY -- TEXT PAGE 338 ~~~~~~~~~~ Division of Decimals

The correct pathway is shown by the dotted line.

```
        Start
1000- - - - - -   10 - - - - - - -   0.1 - - - - - -   100 - - |
1000              1                  0.001             0.01   |
0.001             1                  0.01              10     |
100               100                10                100    |
                                                       END    |
```

ACTIVITY -- TEXT PAGE 339 ~~~~~~~~~~ Diagnostic Help

The problems are modeled with concrete manipulatives:

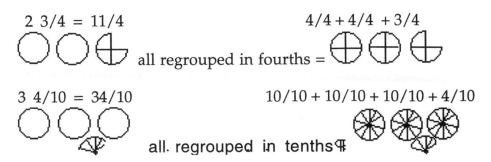

2 3/4 = 11/4   4/4 + 4/4 + 3/4   all regrouped in fourths =

3 4/10 = 34/10   10/10 + 10/10 + 10/10 + 4/10   all. regrouped in tenths

Generalized procedure to get the answers every time:
   Always regroup the whole numbers into the same portions as the fractional part of the problem is using. Then add all

the fractional portions together to form the improper fraction.

ACTIVITY -- TEXT PAGE 340 ~~~~~~~~~ Portfolio Assessments

In the reflective description/analysis of the students' work, the college student should note at least some of the following:

Nick is able to do an algorithm "by rote." Both the drawing and thw word problem indicate Nice does not understand multiplication of fractions. Nick sees 3/4 and 1/2 as separate entities rather than considering the problem as "1/2 **of** 3/4" or "3/4 **of** 1/2."

Dustin does not show that he actually used the division algorithm for fractions. The "defense" of his answer does not really convey any understanding. The drawing in and of itself does not make much sense until you read the word problem. The word problem is a creative problem situation ... and as he stated it, he did reason to a correct solution. However, it doesn't match the stated problem. (3/8 can be viewed as 1/4 plus 1/8 [1/2 of 1/4 of the leftover piece of candy bar.])

Both simply write the problem and answer with no other "work shown."

Neither drawing contains the kind of details that indicate the students are able to model pictorially what they have done abstractly, although Dustin's picture combined with his word problem gives better insight into Dustin's understanding of division of fractions.

In the discussion of assessment standards used, the college student should be able to refer to such understandings as [giving appropriate explanations and/or examples] --
Important, significant mathematics that all students need to know and be able to do (Mathematics Standard)
Allowing students to demonstrate mathematical power in different ways, allowing for individual experiences (Equity Standard)
Communicating understanding, advancing student learning (The Learning Standard)
The college student may indicate other assessment standards as well. As long as the explanation and examples are appropriate to the situation, these should be accepted.

Rubrics may vary somewhat but allow for assessing understanding(s) and processes described above as well as others the college students may have suggested.

ACTIVITY -- TEXT PAGE 341 ~~~~~~~~~~ Assessing
Understanding of Fractions

The college students' answers will vary, but the following are among the insights that may be considered:

There has probably been some exposure to models -- probably fraction circles, but possibly just circles to draw on. Each problem is illustrated with marked/labeled circular shapes.

There is limited conceptual understanding of operations w/fractions -- the models and "work" don't match ... none of the algorithms are appropriately carried through. (It is possible students learned multiplication and division of fractions first since all the problems use the reciprocal of the second fraction in the algorithmic process.)

The instructional processes described will vary but should include one or more concrete models and experiences to develop an understanding of equivalent fractions before algorithmic work is addressed.

While all of the assessment standards are important, the college student will particularly want to include:
The Mathematics Standard, The Learning Standard, and the Equity Standard.

ACTIVITY -- TEXT PAGE 342 ~~~~~~~~~~ Portfolio Assessments

In the reflective description/analysis of the students' work, the college student should note at least some of the following:

Michelle understands the standard multiplication algorithm for whole numbers. She does not seem to understand meaning of decimals or the operation of multiplication with decimals -- she reverts to the whole number model. Further evidence of this is seen in the drawing Michelle uses ... adding 32 fifteen times. The word problem is a whole number, not decimal, situation. Michelle gets the "right" answer for the "wrong" reason.

Danielle indicates an understanding of the standard multiplication of decimals algorithm. It would be helpful if she would show the result of her estimation ($1.20). Michelle indicates an understanding of division as the inverse of multiplication. However, the work as shown makes one wonder if the division of decimals algorithm or the concept of division of decimals is clear (there is no decimal point for the divisor [0.4], the decimal point in the dividend is as it is in the original problem, but the quotient shows the decimal point "moved" one position). The drawing indicates a good sense of place value as well providing evidence of understanding of the algorithm. The word problem is a realistic one.

In the discussion of assessment standards used, the college student should be able to refer to such understandings as [giving appropriate explanations and/or examples] --
Important, significant mathematics that all students need to know and be able to do (Mathematics Standard)
Allowing students to demonstrate mathematical power in different ways, allowing for individual experiences (Equity Standard)
Communicating understanding, advancing student learning (The Learning Standard)
The college student may indicate other assessment standards as well. As long as the explanation and examples are appropriate to the situation, these should be accepted.

Rubrics may vary somewhat but allow for assessing understanding(s) and processes described above as well as others the college students may have suggested.

ENDING EXERCISES -- -- CHAPTER 11

A. MEMORIZATION and COMPREHENSION EXERCISES
Low-Level Thought Activities -- PAGE 343

1. The Cuisenaire rods that equal 1/4 are:

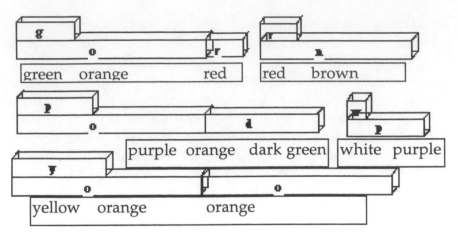

green   orange   red   │ red   brown

purple orange dark green │ white purple

yellow   orange   orange

2. Better terminology = "Express in simplest form" or "rename in lowers terms." Reduce implies "less". The actual concept being stressed is equivalence.

3. The "whole" changes with every fraction considered. Therefore, children must be aware of what unit is being used when comparing one fraction to another.

4. Repeating decimals between 1/2 and 1/10, as shown in unit fractions, are:

   1/3   1/6   1/7   1/9

   Non-terminating, repeating decimals are those that have no ending point on any base 10 number line, but when their decimal equivalents are added together to make one whole, the decimals always add up to 1.

B. APPLICATION and ANALYSIS EXERCISES
Middle-Level Thought Activities -- PAGE 343

1. Answers will vary, depending on the exact examples chosen by the students.
2. Answers will vary, depending on the perceived needs of the students.
3. Answers will vary, depending on the mathematics series chosen by the student.
4. Answers will vary.

C. SYNTHESIS and EVALUATION EXERCISES
High-Level Thought Activities -- PAGE 344

1. }   Answers will vary, depending upon the concept chosen.
2.
3. Answers will vary, but students should be able to summarize their position using the philosophy expressed within the chapter.
4. A remediation plan would include:

a. Analysis of Error Pattern:
   1) The child reads the number from left to right and places the number of zeros to bring the number to the place value normally associated with the whole number system.
   2) The child merely places a decimal point in front of the number, thinking that is all that is needed to show part of a number.

b. Evaluation of Thought Processing
   The same reasoning should be followed here as presented in the ending exercises of Chapter 8 and in #3 in the preceding section for this chapter.

c. Sequential Development
Concrete, remedial ideas appear at the end of this chapter. Their pictorial representation can be drawn by children also.

ACTIVITY ANSWERS -- CHAPTER 12

ACTIVITY -- TEXT PAGE 349 ~~~~~~~~~~ Creating Art Projects
with Percent of Shapes

The activity is self-explanatory.

ACTIVITY -- TEXT PAGE 351 ~~~~~~~~~~ Percent with Pattern
Blocks or Graph Paper

Steps 1 & 3 are shown below. Step 2 will vary depending upon the
pattern blocks and percents chosen. [The graph paper example of
20% is not duplicated.]

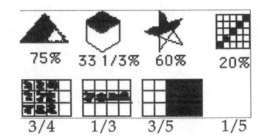

75%   33 1/3%   60%   20%

Fractional equiv.   3/4   1/3   3/5   1/5

ACTIVITY -- TEXT PAGE 352 ~~~~~~~~~~ Analyzing the Steps to
Finding Percents with Computer Programs as Guides

See the CD-ROM section of this instructor's manual.

ACTIVITY -- TEXT PAGE 354 ~~~~~~~~~~ Equivalent Ratios

1. Box 4 and Box 5 show equivalent ratios that are the same as 3:2.
2. The same ratio of 3:2 with Cuisenaire rods:

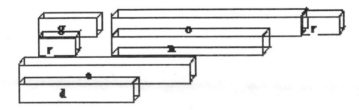

3 - 4. Answers will vary, depending on the manipulatives chosen.

ACTIVITY -- TEXT PAGE 354 ~~~~~~~~~~ Creating Ratios with
Reptiles in Native American Stories

All of the directions for this activity are contained within the
activity on text pages 354-355.

ACTIVITY -- TEXT PAGE 356 ~~~~~~~~~ Origins of Proportional
Relationships

This activity is self-explanatory.

ACTIVITY -- TEXT PAGE 357 ~~~~~~~~~ Creating Your Own
World 10 Times Your Size

This activity is self-explanatory.

ACTIVITY -- TEXT PAGE 357 ~~~~~~~~~ Creating Proportions
with Native American Stories

This activity is self-explanatory.

ACTIVITY -- TEXT PAGE 358 ~~~~~~~~~ Proportions in English

The activity is self-explanatory. All examples should follow the
same format as those which appear in step 2 of the activity.

ACTIVITY -- TEXT PAGE 359 ~~~~~~~~~ Creating Coordinate
Graphs from Other Proportion Examples

See the CD-ROM section of this instructor's manual.

ACTIVITY -- TEXT PAGE 360 ~~~~~~~~~ Finding the Ratio in the
Rate

1. Self-explanatory
2. Answers will vary depending on the examples created by the
student.

ACTIVITY -- TEXT PAGE 362 ~~~~~~~~~ Creating Your Own
Rubric for Percents with Manipulatives

Student answers will vary. Some possible responses they may
make include --
1. All of the children seem to realize to lesser or greater extent that
percent expresses some relation between the parts and the whole.
2. The children do not seem to realize that percent requires equal-
sized pieces for comparisons (fractions, equal parts of whole).
3. Andrew - 20%, 80%; Katelyn - 35%, 47%, 18%; Mark - 32%, 11%,
57%; Justin - 34%, 41%, 24%
Depending on your interpretation, you might argue that Andrew
was the closest, although he did not express his answers as %. but

just gave the number of each part in the picture. Katelyn was closest and her reasoning was logical.

4. This is the type of problem that is well suited to a rubric rating rather than a numerical (% correct) score. An unfamiliar concept, an open-ended task, and a constructed student response all indicate the need for a rubric.

ACTIVITY -- TEXT PAGE 364 ~~~~~~~~~~ Analyzing Child and Adult Knowledge of Percents in Whole Figures

Student answers will vary. Some possible responses they may make include --

1. Each student divided the star(s) into regions.
2. Student A (both); Student B (50%); Student E -- showed positive understandings of percent. Age was not really a significant factor.
3. Some looked only at the arms of the star rather than the totality. Again, age did not seem to be a significant factor.
4. Missing from the adult task -- doing the 50%, a request for an explanation of what was done.
5. Possibly -- doing the 50% task might have been the model that would activate prior knowledge by performing a similar but simpler task first and/or in explaining the process the "error" might have been caught by the adult learner more readily.
   It could also be argued that if the adults did not really understand %, then doing the 50% task and/or explaining the process would have little influence on the given response.

ENDING EXERCISES -- -- CHAPTER 12

A. MEMORIZATION and COMPREHENSION EXERCISES
Low-Level Thought Activities -- PAGE 365

1. Students may reason this way: A $100 item discounted 50% would cost $50. An additional 30% off the discount price would be another $15, for a cost of $35. This is a total discount of $65 or 65%. Or, 30% of 50% is 15%. So the total discount is 65%.
2. Answers will vary.

B. APPLICATION and ANALYSIS EXERCISES
Middle-Level Thought Activities -- PAGE 365

1. Hibernation
    Raindrop
    Cool
2. Answers will vary depending on the textbooks chosen.
3. Answers will vary depending on the textbooks chosen.
4. Answers will vary but could include reference to scale drawings, similar figures, "better buy" comparison, etc.

C. SYNTHESIS and EVALUATION EXERCISES
High-Level Thought Activities -- PAGE 366

1. Answers will vary, depending on the lesson concept chosen.
2. Students need to be aware of the fact that the third year increase would be based on the second year profits. So, for instance, using the example in the text page 351, the small squares would now represent $762.60 (the second year's profit divided by 100).
3. Answers will vary, depending on the example chosen.
4. Answers will vary.

ACTIVITY ANSWERS -- CHAPTER 13

<u>ACTIVITY -- TEXT PAGE 371</u> ~~~~~~~~~ Manipulatives with Odd
and Even Numbers

This activity is self-explanatory.

<u>ACTIVITY -- TEXT PAGE 372</u> ~~~~~~~~~ Addition with Odd and
Even Numbers

Rule:	Rule:	Rule:
When 2 even numbers are added together, the result will be	When 2 odd numbers are added together, the result will be	When an odd and an even number are added together, the result will be
<u>even</u>	<u>even</u>	<u>odd</u>

<u>ACTIVITY -- TEXT PAGE 373</u> ~~~~~~~~~~ The Mystery Even
Number Prime

The answer is contained within the activity itself.

<u>ACTIVITY -- TEXT PAGE 373</u> ~~~~~~~~~~ Number Patterns with
the Sieve of Eratosthenes

Steps 1 through 4 are self-explanatory.

Questions Based on the Sieve of Eratosthenes:
1. Twenty-five or one-fourth of the first 100 numbers are prime.
   The numbers are:
   2, 3, 5, 7, 11, 13, 17, 19, 23, 29, 31, 37, 41, 43, 47, 53, 59, 61, 67, 71, 73, 79, 83, 89, 97
2. Of the first 25 numbers, 29 percent or 2/7 were multiples of three numbers. Of the second 25 numbers, 71 percent or 5/7 were multiples of three numbers.
3. One would expect the number of multiples of three numbers to <u>increase</u> as the total numbers increase in the number system, because more numbers can be multiplied together, thus producing more multiples.
4. Sixty percent or 3/5 of the total primes in the first 100 numbers are found in the first 50 numbers. Forty percent or 2/5 of the total primes in the first 100 numbers are found in the second 50 numbers.

5. By extending the Sieve from 100 to 200 numbers and continuing to find multiples, a person can see that there are less primes (22 to 24 percent) than the first 100 numbers.
6. The first time that a multiple of 7 has not been crossed out is at: 7 x 7 or 7^2
7. It will be at: 11 x 11 or 11^2
8. The first time that a multiple of any number will not be crossed out by a multiple of a smaller prime is at the point that the given number is squared, i.e., multiplied by itself.

ACTIVITY -- TEXT PAGE 375 ~~~~~~~~~ Finding the LCM and
GCF with Cuisenaire Rods

Answers will vary according to the examples chosen by students.

ACTIVITY -- TEXT PAGE 376 ~~~~~~~~~ Achievement Test
Simulation

It is important that students do these problems MENTALLY and without the benefit of a calculator to simulate the common standardized testing situation where no calculator is allowed. Encourage students to do the test again after studying the divisibility rules.

ACTIVITY -- TEXT PAGE 377 ~~~~~~~~~ Divisibility by 4 and 8

The answer is contained within the activity.

ACTIVITY -- TEXT PAGE 378 ~~~~~~~~~ Pythagoras and History

This activity is self-explanatory.

ACTIVITY -- TEXT PAGE 379 ~~~~~~~~~ Triples

Triple	Theorem
6 8 10	36 + 64 = 100
	100 = 100
9 12 15	81 + 144 = 225
	225 = 225
12 16 20	144 + 256 = 400
	400 = 400
15 20 25	225 + 400 = 625
	625 = 625
18 24 30	324 + 576 = 900
	900 = 900

To generalize a rule:
Any multiple of the starting triple will fit the formula for the Pythagorean Triples.

ACTIVITY -- TEXT PAGE 380 ~~~~~~~~~~ Music and Science with Fibonacci Numbers

Answers will vary depending on individual interests.

ACTIVITY -- TEXT PAGE 381 ~~~~~~~~~~ Pascal's Triangle

1. Level 8 will have 9 spaces: 1 8 __ __ __ __ __ 8 1
   Level 9 will have 10 spaces: 1 9 __ __ __ __ __ __ 9 1
2. The second and third number on each side when added together make the third number in the next row. The same pattern is seen between the third and fourth number of each set, etc. to generate the fourth number in the next level.

   The numbers are filled in on each level through level 7, 8, and 9:

   Numbers Added Per Row

   start
level													Numbers Added Per Row
level 1						1							2
level 2					1	2	1						4
level 3				1	3	3	1						8
level 4			1	4	6	4	1						16
level 5		1	5	10	10	5	1						32
level 6	1	6	15	20	15	6	1						64
level 7	1	7	21	35	35	21	7	1					128
level 8	1	8	28	56	70	56	28	8	1				256
level 9	1	9	36	84	126	126	84	36	9	1			512

3. When the numbers in each row are added together, they represent 2 to the nth power, where n equals the number of each level of triangle.
4. The formula is equal to the definition which appears in step 3.

ACTIVITY -- TEXT PAGE 383 ~~~~~~~~~~ The History of Negative Numbers

This activity is self-explanatory.

ACTIVITY -- TEXT PAGE 384 ~~~~~~~~~~ Economics

Directions for using this activity with elementary and middle school students are explained within the activity itself. No answers are required here.

ACTIVITY -- TEXT PAGE 385 ~~~~~~~~~~ Get a Charge out of
Integers

Answers are given within the activity itself.

ACTIVITY -- TEXT PAGE 387 ~~~~~~~~~~ Simultaneous Equations
with Middle School Interests in Mind

Directions for using this activity with elementary and middle
school students are explained within the activity itself. No answers
are required here.

ACTIVITY -- TEXT PAGE 390 ~~~~~~~~~~ Graphing Calculator
with Equations

No answers are required here.

ACTIVITY -- TEXT PAGE 391 ~~~~~~~~~~ Origins of Algebraic
Concepts

No answers are required here.

ACTIVITY -- TEXT PAGE 392 ~~~~~~~~~~ Portfolio Assessments

Student answers will vary.   Some possible responses they may
make include --
2. All of the children looked for patterns. All could explain their
   pattern continuation in a way that had some relationship to the
   starting sequence.
   Matthew and Mark (both 8) - Mark uses higher order thinking in
   looking at stair steps pattern rather than matching colors (and
   thus reversing the sequence).
   Kate and Mark (both 3rd grade) - Mark's doubling within the
   sequence rather than at the end is more in keeping with the
   patterning concept.

ACTIVITY -- TEXT PAGE 394 ~~~~~~~~~~ Portfolio Assessments

This activity refers to Figures 13.25 and 13.26. Figure 13.25 is Greg's
work, he is eight years old. Figure 13.26 is Kate's work, she is 9 years
old.
Student answers will vary.   Some possible responses they may
make include --

Both recognize "the rule." Greg states the rule in simplest form and does not draw examples. Kate not only states the rule, she draws possible outcomes.

ACTIVITY -- TEXT PAGE 394 ~~~~~~~~~ Portfolio Assessments

Student answers will vary. Some possible responses they may make include --
Travis' work seems to indicate that his experiences have been of the abstract/symbolic, rote type.
Had Travis had experiences with manipulatives, he might have been able to make connections to the real world, known at least 2 ways to validate his solutions, not have gotten the right answer when making the mistake he made at the end of the first part of his work, might have demonstrated how he found the second set of answers.
Travis knows that you need to find solutions for x and y. He seems to believe that there is a certain number/particular order of steps that have to be used. He doesn't seem to know what relation a linear equation has to real world experiences.

ENDING EXERCISES -- -- CHAPTER 13

A. MEMORIZATION and COMPREHENSION EXERCISES
Low-Level Thought Activities -- PAGE 396

1. Answers will vary, depending on the student's own words. Each rule should follow the directions given in the text.
2. The number is divisible by all except 5 and 10.
3. The number is divisible by 5 and 10 if zero is added as the last digit: 9468720

B. APPLICATION and ANALYSIS EXERCISES
Middle-Level Thought Activities -- PAGE 396

1. Answers will vary, depending on the number patterns found.
2. The number, 19711, is between the squares of the primes 139 and 149.
    139 x 139 = 19321   149 x 149 = 22201
    The next lowest prime below 139 is 137, so the test will start there.
    Using a calculator, divide 19711 by each lower prime, namely -- 137, 133, 131, 127, 113, 109, 107, 103, 101, 97, 89, 83, 79, 73, 71, 67, 61, 59, 53, 47, 43, 41, 37, 31, 29, 23

All the quotients are decimals until the prime, 23, is tried.
The whole number, 857, is the quotient. This proves that 23
is a factor of 19711, so 19711 is NOT a prime number.
3. A divisibility rule for 6 is easy to see. If a number fits the
divisibility rule for 2 <u>and</u> 3, then the number is also divisible by
6.
A divisibility rule for 7, and one for 11, are not presented here,
because they are included as high level test items for this
chapter. Answers to high level test questions are seen at the end
of each set of test items in the last section of this instructor's
manual.
4. The prediction of differences may vary, depending on student's
mathematical language and knowledge.

$$4x + y = 10 \qquad 4x - y = 10$$

x	y	x	y
2	2	2	-2
1	6	1	-6
0	10	0	-10

In each equation, if $y = 0$, $4x = 10$ ---> $x = 2.5$

C. SYNTHESIS and EVALUATION EXERCISES
<u>High-Level Thought Activities</u> -- PAGE 396

1. Any base that has an odd number of individual units in its
LONG or 10 will not be able to "pair" the individual units;
therefore, making 10 an odd number in that base as seen on the
next page:

Base three   Base seven
     Base five   Base nine

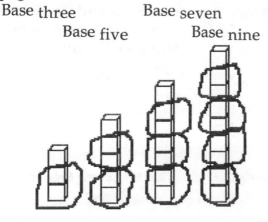

2. Primes = 1, 10., 11, 101, 111, 1011, 1101 in base two.
3. Answers will vary depending upon the concept chosen.

ACTIVITY ANSWERS -- CHAPTER 14

ACTIVITY -- TEXT PAGE 405 ~~~~~~~~~~ Native American
Pictographs

This activity is self-explanatory.

ACTIVITY -- TEXT PAGE 405 ~~~~~~~~~~ Picture Graph

No answers are needed here.

ACTIVITY -- TEXT PAGE 406 ~~~~~~~~~~ Favorite Academic
Subject

The answers are contained in the activity itself.

ACTIVITY -- TEXT PAGE 408 ~~~~~~~~~~ Plotting Continuous
Line Graphs in Science

A. Conclusion: Speed starts quickly, levels out over time and accelerates near the finish of a time sequence.

B. Conclusion: Speed accelerates over time, gradually leveling out as time slows to a constant rate.

C. Conclusion: Speed slows as time advances.

D. Conclusion: Speed accelerates and decelerates at an uneven pace as time continues to advance.

ACTIVITY -- TEXT PAGE 408 ~~~~~~~~~~ More Practice with
Plotting Line Graphs in Science

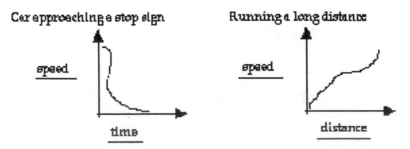

ACTIVITY -- TEXT PAGE 410 ~~~~~~~~~~ Story Writing with
Scatter Graphs

2-3.   Answers will vary, depending on the newspaper story
chosen.

4-5. The scaling key for each graph has changed but the information
has not changed. Therefore, the newspaper story is the same, but
its perception to the public reading the story may have changed
from the different impression left by each graph.
In Graph II the space given to the X scale points has been
widened while the space given to the Y scale points has been
shortened.
In Graph III the space given to the X scale points has been
shortened while the space given to the Y scale points has been
widened.

ACTIVITY -- TEXT PAGE 412 ~~~~~~~~~~Cultural Contributions to
Statistics and Probability

This activity is self-explanatory.

ACTIVITY -- TEXT PAGE 412 ~~~~~~~~~~ Mean

The answer is found within the example given.

ACTIVITY -- TEXT PAGE 414 ~~~~~~~~~~ Native American Lesson
on Natural Resources with Statistics

This activity is self-explanatory.

ACTIVITY -- TEXT PAGE 417 ~~~~~~~~~~ Coin Toss

H:To => 16:30   Ta:To => 14:30   H:Ta => 16:14.

ACTIVITY -- TEXT PAGE 417 ~~~~~~~~~~ Die Toss

1-2. Answers will vary, depending on the toss of the die.
The theoretical probabilities are:
3. Each number appears 1/6 or 16.66 throws in 100 throws.
4. A number less than 3 occurs 2/6 or 1/3 of the time.

5. An odd number occurs 3/6 or 1/2 of the time.
6. A prime number occurs 3/6 or 1/2 of the time.
   A multiple of 3 occurs 2/6 or 1/3 of the time.
   A multiple of 2 occurs 3/6 or 1/2 of the time.

ACTIVITY -- TEXT PAGE 418 ~~~~~~~~~~ Probabilities with Cards

The answer is found within the example given.

ACTIVITY -- TEXT PAGE 418 ~~~~~~~~~~ Tree Diagram

The answer is found within the example given.

ACTIVITY -- TEXT PAGE 419 ~~~~~~~~~~ Probability Path

Answers will vary depending on the toss of the die by the
individual students. The boxes in the middle will yield a greater
percentage of the tosses because the arrangement of the odd and
even boxes favors the middle positions with less of a percentage as
the boxes go toward the outside. The distribution is in the shape of
the bell curve, the normal distribution in statistics.

ACTIVITY -- TEXT PAGE 420 ~~~~~~~~~~ Science

Answers will vary, depending on the student's individual
experiment. All things being equal, the length of the pencil in
relation to the parallel lines remains the same since the lines are
always 1.5 times the length of the pencil being used.

ACTIVITY -- TEXT PAGE 424 ~~~~~~~~~~ Permutations with
                                              Letters

The answer is found within the example given.
Other situations where permutations can be used are in license
plates, Lotto games, etc.

ACTIVITY -- TEXT PAGE 424 ~~~~~~~~~~ Exploring Combinations

The answer is found within the example given.

ACTIVITY -- TEXT PAGE 426 ~~~~~~~~~~ Creating Your Own
Rubric for Continuous Graphs

Student answers will vary. Some possible responses they may make
include --
Both Mark and Kate related something to each part of the graph.
Mark doesn't see relationships within the graph; he considers
elements in isolation (e.g., time for clock; arrows point to numbers).
Kate doesn't think through the initial acceleration (at least I hope
cars don't come out of driveways so quickly); she starts immediately
with a story rather than identifying relationships of the parts of the
graph.
Again, this is the type of problem that calls for a rubric.

ACTIVITY -- TEXT PAGE 426 ~~~~~~~~~~ Creating Your Own
Rubric for Averages

Student answers will vary. Some possible responses they may make
include --
Both students attemped to answer each question. They both
understand average as some type of relationship to a set of
numbers.
Student #1 sees average as algorithm.
Student #2 sees average as mode.
(Table 14.2, text page 427, details this quite well.)
An argument for a numerical score might be made here by some
college students ... probably with the idea of multiple points so that
partial credit could be given. A rubric could also be used, especially
given the explanation that was to be provided. The instructor will
have to consider the reasoning of the college students in this. What
Student #2 doesn't say in the explanation is why s/he ordered the
numbers in attendance but not in the first two sets of numbers.

ENDING EXERCISES -- -- CHAPTER 14

A. MEMORIZATION and COMPREHENSION EXERCISES
Low-Level Thought Activities -- PAGE 429

1. Use any computer graphing program to complete these graphs.
2. Answers will vary.
3. Answers will vary.

4. Answers will vary.

B. APPLICATION and ANALYSIS EXERCISES
Middle-Level Thought Activities -- PAGE 429

1. Answers will vary, depending on the articles found.
2. Answers will vary but should be in keeping with the philosophy of the NCTM Standards and this chapter. Such reasons as real world relevance, developing critical thinking skills, making reasonable choices in probability situations are appropriate.

C. SYNTHESIS and EVALUATION EXERCISES
High-Level Thought Activities -- PAGE 429

1. Answers will vary, depending on the topic and the lesson chosen.
2. A number of good computer spreadsheet programs can be used for this activity. The students will need to check the documentation for the respective program when constructing their own spreadsheets.
3. Answers will vary depending upon the lesson/literature chosen.
4. Answer will vary. The game in the text can be used as a model but the student's newly constructed game should be different from the one on text page 419.

LESSONS LEARNED IN ACCESSING THE CD-ROM

SOME GENERAL COMMENTS

First of all, I have to say how much I like having some actual classroom scenes, with talking children and teachers. These short snippets are ideal for focusing in on one particular aspect or facet of the teaching/learning process. The multicultural scenarios are also greatly appreciated since many of my students often have not had experiences in those types of settings. Much of what follows is a repeat of the documentation that is provided with the CD-ROM but I suspect more than a few of you have skipped some of the documentation reading. So, here are a few reminders and helpful hints.

THE VIDEO VIGNETTES

Everything you need to access the CD-ROM version of the text with the extended activities and video vignettes is contained on the CD-ROM. The same CD-ROM can be accessed in either a Windows or a Macintosh machine. As a matter of fact, when I popped the CD into an IBM, the directions for installing the Acrobat Reader program came up automatically. This was looking like a superior user-friendly piece of work. However, what does not come up automatically is the reminder to also copy the movie plug-in into the Acrobat Reader plug-in folder. Needless to say, I didn't even think about that.

When I tried to play a video vignette from within the CD-book, all I would get was a little gray box with a big fat question mark in it! For the life of me, I couldn't figure out what was wrong. But I did try running the movie clip directly through the QuickTime movie player, and that worked just fine. (In case you haven't guessed by now, my computer of choice is the MAC and since I was operating with one of the very first cuts of the CD, I didn't have external documentation to refer to. And, being the impatient kind, I skimmed, and yes, occasionally skipped, the on-line documentation. It really is a good idea to read the "Read me" files!)

The movie clips really do work best if you keep the size of the video relatively small. I found as I enlarged the frame, the picture began to get fuzzy and occasionally the sound would skip a bit. The other thing to remember is that all of my "playing" has been on home, desk-top models. I suspect that will be true for most of the students and many of you who are using this CD as well.

Whether you're running the CD on a MAC or an IBM, you really do need at least 16 megs of RAM. I was running it with 12 meg for the first few days and the sound track was really distorted. If that's all you have, then you will get better sound if you copy a clip to your hard drive and run it directly through QuickTime's Movie Player. Of course, the movie clips are memory intensive, and I could only copy one clip at a time onto my hard drive. When I had finished with that one, I "trashed" it and copied the next one onto the hard drive. (When I finally plunged in and upgraded to 36 megs of RAM, the clarity of the sound track was incredible.)

THE EXTENDED ACTIVITIES

There is a wealth of materials that provide students with opportunities for independent exploration or ideas for creating units and lessons for their own teaching. Occasionally, you will want to print something out. Be sure and specify a page range -- the page range from the CD ... not the text! If you don't specify a page range, you will get almost 1100 pages of print. If you specify page numbers from the text, you will probably not get what you are expecting.

There are a few places where we got ahead of ourselves with the technology. Anytime I came across missing items, or strange integrations of different assignments, I tried to remember to note that at that very spot in the instructor's manual. Where possible, we have provided alternate materials in the instructor's manual that you can print out for your students to use.

As you come across "glitches" that we have missed, please leave us a message at our web site. There's a great deal of excitement when you venture out on the cutting edge, but we also know that we are only human and have probably missed a few items here and there. Enjoy the adventure of the technology and let us hear from you!

J. A. M.

CHAPTER 1

EXTENDED EXERCISES

The extended activities in this first chapter do not require any answers in this manual.

LOGO ACTIVITY -- ESTIMATING THE SIZE OF THE LOGO SCREEN

The illustration below shows the range of turtle steps that would be considered a reasonable estimate. Any answer within or close to this range should be considered correct.

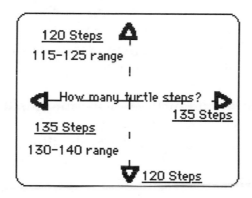

EXTENDED ENDING EXERCISES

A. MEMORIZATION and COMPREHENSION EXERCISES
Low-Level Thought Activities

1. There are many areas from which to choose the five . . .
   - a. Technology
   - b. Position Papers
   - c. Estimation
   - d. Manipulatives
   - e. Mathematical Connections
   - f. Mental Math
   - g. Problem Solving
   - h. Cultural Relevance

2. Answers will vary.
3. Answers will vary.
4. Answers will vary, depending on the specific book on the history of mathematics that was chosen.

B. APPLICATION and ANALYSIS EXERCISES
Middle-Level Thought Activities

1. Articles chosen will vary, depending on the journals used for the reviews.
2. Answers will vary.

C. SYNTHESIS and EVALUATION EXERCISES
High-Level Thought Activities

1. Answers will vary, but the position needs to be justified based on the evidence provided in the review of the literature.

2. Answers will vary, but the major thrust should refer to the compatibility of learning computation and the appropriate use of calculators. At this time, the Standards call for a lesser emphasis, not an elimination, on time-consuming, rote computation.

3-4. The response should include ideas from the the NCTM Information Sheets/Position Papers as well as other points from the student's reading and review of the literature.

5. Answers will vary, depending on the position taken by each college student.

6. The five goals of the NCTM curriculum standards are:
   a. Becoming a mathematical problem solver
   b. Learning to communicate mathematically
   c. Learning to reason mathematically
   d. Valuing mathematics
   e. Becoming confident in one's ability to do mathematics.

   Answers by the college students will vary on how classroom instruction can help these goals.

CHAPTER 2

EXTENDED ACTIVITY ANSWERS

The extended activities in this second chapter do not require any answers in this manual.

The format for responding to the questions about the video vignette can be found in the text, pages 58 and 59. The NCTM teaching standards that support this lesson (or vice versa) are found in the text on page 66.

EXTENDED ENDING EXERCISES

A. MEMORIZATION and COMPREHENSION EXERCISES
Low-Level Thought Activities

1. C -- -- Concrete manipulations

2. Piaget

3. Answers will vary because the students are to use their own words for the definition.

4. The stages of each theorist are found on text pages 29 to 35. All have stages which go from the first steps of concrete, physical manipulations to the last steps of abstract, symbolic representation where only mental transformations are necessary. Some of the stages are age-related while others spiral from one stage to another for each new concept at any age.

5. (1) Constructivist, (2) Behaviorist, (3) Information Processing. The major contributions of each school are found on text pages 29 to 45.

6. Answers will vary, depending on the elementary or middle school textbook that is chosen.

7. 1. Understand the problem and be motivated to answer it.
   2. Know facts and strategies useful in solving the problem; devise a plan.

3. Apply various strategies until the problem is solved; carry out the plan.
4. Check the solution to see if it is correct.
    These four steps of Polya's can be found in both Chapter 1 and Chapter 2.

B. APPLICATION and ANALYSIS EXERCISES
Middle-Level Thought Activities

1. Answers will vary, depending on the elementary or middle school textbook page chosen.
2. The three ways may be adapted from those seen on text page 39, or new ways may be created by the student.
3. Answers will vary, but important components would include an awareness of brain research, multiple intelligences theories, learning theories and learning styles, the importance of problem solving, and the integration of curriculum through mathematics.
4.-5. Answers will vary, depending on the particular software and/or topics chosen.

C. SYNTHESIS and EVALUATION EXERCISES
High-Level Thought Activities

1. Answers will vary, depending on the textbook series chosen.

3. Answers will vary, depending on the lesson/teacher observed.

4. Answers will vary, depending on the teacher interviewed.

5. The question is to be used as an essay over the important points covered in the chapter. Each instructor may wish to set his/her own standard for the number of points and content to be covered in an acceptable essay. Answers will vary, but included in the response should be the idea that children learn mathematics by doing mathematics and that most children learn best by beginning at the concrete level in developing understanding.

CHAPTER 3

EXTENDED ACTIVITY ANSWERS

<u>ACTIVITY -- -- BLACK HISTORY CONNECTIONS</u>

Five ways that this unit can be connected to middle school
mathematics topics might include:
Geometry ... patterns, tesselations
Measurement ... area, perimeter, scale (ratio, proportion), percent
The college students may have other topics that they would
recommend.
The activities will vary, depending on the topics chosen.

The remaining activities in this chapter need no answers here A
comment on the LOGO program, GOSHAPES2 -- it will run faster if
you hide the turtle before running the program. A sample printout
is given below, but the multi-colored drawing within the program
is far prettier than this.

The following shape was created by GOSHAPES 2:

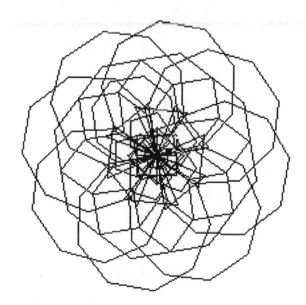

EXTENDED ENDING EXERCISES

A. MEMORIZATION and COMPREHENSION EXERCISES
Low-Level Thought Activities

1. Questions asked: <u>How can we take students from culturally-diverse backgrounds and give them the mathematical understanding needed to be full participants in society? How much does the presence of diverse cultural backgrounds and beliefs play in the acquisition of mathematics understanding?</u>
2. Wording may vary, but students should point to research involving technology, particularly computers; LEP studies; MAC-mathics Program work, etc.

B. APPLICATION and ANALYSIS EXERCISES
Middle-Level Thought Activities

1. Answers will vary, depending on the software chosen.
2. Answers will vary, depending on the journals and textbooks selected.

C. SYNTHESIS and EVALUATION EXERCISES
High-Level Thought Activities

1-5. Answers will vary.

CHAPTER 4

EXTENDED ACTIVITY ANSWERS

ACTIVITY -- -- Modeling Subtraction and its Meaning

Students may have a variety of suggestions including the following. Taylor: Have her estimate the answer. Have her check using addition. Use concrete materials such as base ten blocks in a take-away model. (It is important for the college students to understand that in a take-away model, only the minuend is modeled with the blocks. The subtrahend is taken from the minuend model.) Mikolas: is making the "error" described above ... in the take-away model, only the minuend is modeled with the blocks. He is using the blocks, but still does not seem to understand place value and its role in the subtraction process.

ACTIVITY -- -- Number Sense Using Benchmarks

Answers will vary.

ACTIVITY -- -- Create the Graph

Answers will vary. The use of the open-ended performance task is a change from traditional assessment methods.

ACTIVITY -- -- Hidden Digits

Answers will vary, but may include such ideas as knowledge of basic facts, reasoning, strategies for solving, algorthmic knowledge.

Students should notice that the addition and multiplication problems have only one solution:

```
   322              338
   627            x  24
   949            1352
                  6760
                  8112
```

The subtraction problem has many solutions: 3701 - 345 = 3356; 3801 - 445 = 3356; 3791 - 441 = 3350 are just three.

EXTENDED ENDING EXERCISES

A. MEMORIZATION and COMPREHENSION EXERCISES
Low-Level Thought Activities

1. A rubric is the scoring guide used in assessment. It is based on the criteria or qualities desired in the assessment task. Rubrics are sets of criteria that describe levels of performance or understanding. Rubrics provide students with expectations about what will be assessed as well as standards that need to be met; increase consistency in the rating of performances, products and understandings; and provide students with "road signs" -- information about where they are in relation to where they need to be.

2. A portfolio is a carefully designed or purposeful collection or body of work demonstrating the mathematical progress and/or mathematical power of a given student. It most often represents those mathematical endeavors most valued as important indicators of student learning.

B. APPLICATION and ANALYSIS EXERCISES
Middle-Level Thought Activities

1.-2. Answers will vary.

C. SYNTHESIS and EVALUATION EXERCISES
High-Level Thought Activities

1.-2. Answers will vary.

CHAPTER 5

EXTENDED ACTIVITY ANSWERS

ACTIVITY -- -- Geoboard Explorations

Answers will vary.

ACTIVITY -- -- Working on Nets

Answers will vary, depending on the objects brought from home.

ACTIVITY -- -- Mirror Transformations

Answers will vary, depending on the objects and patterns created. Note to the instructor: The last question in #3 should ask, "How many lines ..."

ACTIVITY -- -- Tangram Quilts

This activity is similar to one of the activities in the geoboard exploration of area and perimeter. The student should be finding the Pythagorean Theorem.

ACTIVITY -- -- Making Quilts Shows our Culture

No answers are needed here.

ACTIVITY -- -- Geometry Tells the Story

No answers are needed here.

VIDEO VIGNETTE -- Shape Sorting

This vignette is movie clip 5a. The opening sequence is Dr. Mary Hatfield demonstrating a concept for her methods students.

In the classroom sequence, the first girl seen is an example of the student described by Dr. Hatfield in the opening ... one who believes that for a figure to be a triangle, it must be a certain type, and in a certain orientation. The second girl in the sequence seems to be uncertain of the name of the shape ("It's a sandwich.") but is able to gather all of the triangles rather easily once the teacher gives her the name of the shape. The first boy, in the red shirt, picked up all the triangles easily. The boy in the black shirt was able to sort the triangles easily but was uncertain about rectangles and squares.

Students responses to the follow-up assessment and instructional activities will vary but should be in keeping with the philosophy of this chapter and the NCTM Standards.

ACTIVITY -- Area of 4

Directions are contained within the activity. There are many, but only a finite number, of different shapes that can be created on the geoboard having an area of 4 square units.

ACTIVITY -- Perimeter of 30

Directions are contained within the activity. Designs, and reflections on the results, will vary.

ACTIVITY -- Possible or Impossible

All but number 4 are possible on a geoboard. Students may sketch a number of possible figures meeting the criteria. One example of each is given below.

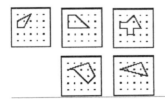

VIDEO VIGNETTE -- Finding Pic's Theorem

This vignette is movie clip 5. The opening sequence is Dr. Mary Hatfield demonstrating a concept for her methods students. I believe the title is somewhat misleading since the students are not actually working to discover Pic's Theorem in this part of the class sequence.

In the classroom sequence, the boy seems to have the beginning of an understanding that the area of triangles is 1/2 the area of the rectangle created by 2 (congruent) triangles, one of which is "flipped over" so that the hypotenuse becomes a line of symmetry.

Students' responses to the types of activities that might be beneficial for the student and reflective analysis of the teaching and learning observed will vary. The types of activities should be in keeping with the philosophy of the chapter. Some students might observe that perhaps the classroom teacher is doing a little too much work for the student in this discovery phase ... the ability to give hints to approaches without giving away the path is a narrow line to walk.

ACTIVITY -- What did You Discover?

The children's work that was supposed to have been included for this activity was inadvertently omitted from the CD. The following children's work can be printed and duplicated if the instructor wishes to use this activity. Or, it may be used as an end of chapter assessment item.

The students whose work is shown below are all fourth graders.

Namu **Sammy**

1. Use one trapezoid and three triangles to make a hexagon.

2. Use three rhombus pieces to make a hexagon.

3. Are the hexagons in #1 and #2 congruent? Explain why you think they are or are not congruent.

   I think they are becaues they both have the same and size the only think is they don't have the same lines in the middel

4. Trace the yellow hexagon in the space below. Use a ruler to draw all the lines of symmetry you can find. How many lines of symmetry did you draw?

   9

Name __Juanita__

1. Use one trapezoid and three triangles
   to make a hexagon.

2. Use three rhombus pieces to make a hexagon.

3. Are the hexagons in #1 and #2 congruent?
   Explain why you think they are or are not congruent.

   *yes & no, they are both hexagons, but they
   are made up of different shapes.*

4. Trace the yellow hexagon in the space below. Use a
   ruler to draw all the lines of symmetry you can find.
   How many lines of symmetry did you draw?

12

Name ___Sabrina___

1. Use one trapezoid and three triangles
   to make a hexagon.

2. Use three rhombus pieces to make a hexagon.

3. Are the hexagons in #1 and #2 congruent?
   Explain why you think they are or are not congruent.

   *I do think these hexagons in number 1 & 2 are
   congruent because they are both hexagons & it
   doesn't matter what blocks you use*

4. Trace the yellow hexagon in the space below. Use a
   ruler to draw all the lines of symmetry you can find.
   How many lines of symmetry did you draw?

   4 lines of symmetry

Name   __Khan__

1. Use one trapezoid and three triangles
   to make a hexagon.

2. Use three rhombus pieces to make a hexagon.

3. Are the hexagons in #1 and #2 congruent?
   Explain why you think they are or are not congruent.

   *Because if you folded them it would not
   be congruent.*

4. Trace the yellow hexagon in the space below. Use a
   ruler to draw all the lines of symmetry you can find.
   How many lines of symmetry did you draw?

 3

EXTENDED ENDING EXERCISES

A. MEMORIZATION and COMPREHENSION EXERCISES
Low-Level Thought Activities

1. A net is the pattern that can be made by covering a three-dimensional figure in paper without any overlapping pieces. Nets are helpful in understanding the relationship between two- and three-dimensional figures. Nets are also helpful in improving the perception of spatial relationships.
2. Some possible uses of geoboards include: symmetry, area, perimeter, fractions, create shapes, create patterns, classification, coordinate geometry.

B. APPLICATION and ANALYSIS EXERCISES
Middle-Level Thought Activities

1. Answers will vary, but each point should be supported by clear justifications based on the concepts and research covered in this chapter.
2. Answers will vary, depending on the software selected.

C. SYNTHESIS and EVALUATION EXERCISES
High-Level Thought Activities

1. Answers will vary, but the comparisons made should be supported with examples drawn from reading and experience. Both geoboards and pentominoes provide perceptual cues. Making pentominoes is more difficult for younger children, but once made can be less abstract than geoboard figures. Pentominoes do not lend themselves easily to perimeter or area of figures other than quadrilaterals. The size of figures that can be made is somewhat limited with the geoboard. The geoboard can be easily used by both field-dependent and field-independent learners when studying area of triangles.
2. Lessons plans will vary, depending upon the activities chosen.
3. The question is used as an essay over the important points covered in the chapter. Each instructor may set his/her own standard for the number of points and content to be covered in an acceptable essay.

CHAPTER 6

EXTENDED ACTIVITY ANSWERS

ACTIVITY -- --   Map Scales in Social Studies

Answers will vary depending on the cities chosen.

ACTIVITY -- --   Metric Measurements

Directions are given in the activity.

CAUTION: A typical error made by some students is to forget to halve the number of pages in the book because one actual page equals two pages of printed matter. The student needs to figure the thickness of actual pages.

ACTIVITY -- --   Estimation with Graph Paper

Rectangles are arranged from least to greatest area. One pattern to be seen is the greater the length and the lesser the width, the lesser the area. As the length diminishes by a centimeter and the width becomes greater by a centimeter, the area becomes greater.

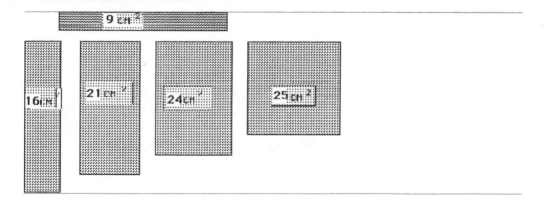

ACTIVITY -- --   Metric Measurement with Area

After experimenting the formula should show that the number of square meters laid side by side along one length and one width of the room can be multiplied together to find the total square meters that could fill the floor (surface area) of the room.

ACTIVITY -- --   Using a Table and Square Centimeters

The measured area is the part which appears here:

Object	Measure Area in cm^2
a quarter	4.91 cm^2
bottom of a 1 lb coffee tin	81.67 cm^2
3x5 index card (7.6 cm x 12.6 cm)	95.76 cm^2
your closed hand	
heel on your shoe	
a picture of a lake	Answers will vary.
surface area of a block	
surface area of a pyramid	

ACTIVITY -- --   Using Volume

Answers will vary depending on the individual's height and average body measurements.

ACTIVITY -- --   Social Studies and Science

Answers will vary depending on the cities chosen by the students.

ACTIVITY -- --   Cuisenaire Rod Clock

Explanation and directions for the activity appear within the activity.

SPREADSHEET ACTIVITY -- -- Metric Table Spreadsheet

The formulas appear under the appropriate prefix for metric measures:

=== A ====	B ====	C ====	D =====	E =====	F =====	G =====
KILO	HECTO	DEKA	UNIT	DECI	CENTI	MILLI
+D3/1000	+D3/100	+D3/10	1	+D3*10	+D3*100	+D3*1000

SPREADSHEET -- -- Calculating with a Spreadsheet

The spreadsheet categories can be calculated by each column using the formulas to correspond to the correct cells in the spreadsheet.

Answers:

Area	Radius	Diameter
379.98 cm²	11.000579 cm	22.001158 cm
256.78 cm²	9.043068 cm	18.086135 cm
307101.9 cm²	312.735 cm	625.47 cm
385 cm²	11.07302 cm	22.14601 cm
3215.36 cm²	32 cm	64 cm
1771.156 cm²	23.75 cm	47.5 cm
221.5584 cm²	8.4 cm	16.8 cm

SPREADSHEET ACTIVITY -- -- Exploring Circles with Spreadsheets

To find the area within listening range of the WKYK station:
Known:

Other information that can be determined:

diameter $2r = 2(50) = 100$ km

circumference $2\pi r = 2 (3.14)(50) = 3$

area $= \pi^2 = (3.14)(50)(50) = 7850$ km

There are a variety of ways of setting up the spreadsheet. Examples of formulas for the spreadsheet, where the radius is entered in cell B1 . . .

in cell F1	2*B1
in cell F2	+B1^ 2*3.14
in cell F3	2*3.14*B1

VIDEO VIGNETTE -- Portfolio Assessments

In the classroom sequence, the girl in the striped shirt appears to be counting the sections as instructed by the teacher; the girl in the plaid shirt seems to be counting pegs ... at one point she says the perimeter is 13. The boy in the blue shirt appeared to be making a triangular shape and counting the sections inside the shape (area) instead of the perimeter. The girl in the yellow dress seems to be counting the sections.

Student responses to the steps to correct misconceptions and the rubric for evaluation will vary but should be in keeping with the philosophy of this chapter and the NCTM Standards.

EXTENDED ENDING EXERCISES

A. MEMORIZATION and COMPREHENSION EXERCISES
Low-Level Thought Activities

1. Answers will vary.
2. Examples of various activities using the measurement model for linear measurement, capacity, volume, and mass have been shown in the chapter. Students may vary the experiments but allow the conclusions to be the same as those proven in the text.
3. Answers will vary, but the main advantages and disadvantages mentioned in the chapter should be present in the student's list.
4. Answers will vary, depending on the textbook series chosen.

B. APPLICATION and ANALYSIS EXERCISES
Middle-Level Thought Activities

1-5. Answers will vary, depending on the topic or examples chosen.
6. The audio-visual library of the college or university should have the materials needed or be able to share catalogs from which the students can see the offerings available in the area of measurement.
7-8. Answers will vary, depending on the topic, textbook series, and/or grade level chosen.

C. SYNTHESIS and EVALUATION EXERCISES
High-Level Thought Activities

1-2. These two exercises require the college students to develop a unit (series of lessons) on a concept of their choice. Alignment with the measurement curriculum and objectives (assuming the same grade level is chosen for both questions) would be expected. Continuity between lessons with review at the start of each new lesson is important and should be seen in the students' work.
3. Answers will vary, depending on the grade level selected for this activity. More challenging lessons should be seen for upper grade children stressing decimal relationships and multi-step strategies among the variables of money, metric measure, and numeration.
4. Answers will vary, depending on the topic and software selected.

CHAPTER 7

EXTENDED ACTIVITY ANSWERS

All of the extended activities in this chapter are self-explanatory.

EXTENDED ENDING EXERCISES

A. MEMORIZATION and COMPREHENSION EXERCISES
Low-Level Thought Activities

1. The answer is   seriation.

2. Types of Counting: Examples:
   Rote Counting
   Rational Counting   Answers will vary.
   Counting with Meaning

3. Manipulatives that can be used to teach children patterns:
   a. Connecting cubes
      Different color patterns
      Vertical or horizontal positioning, etc.
   b. Attribute blocks ...(see Appendix C for patterns)
   c. Stickers on cards
   d. Pattern blocks in red, green, blue, and yellow
      Two examples showing patterns with color and shape:

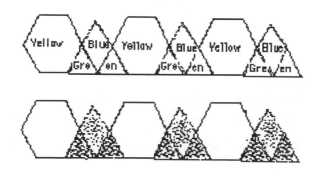

These are just a few of the more prominent materials used to teach patterning. There are many more from which students may choose.

4. Answers will vary, depending on the kind of instruction each person had as a child in the school system.

B. APPLICATION and ANALYSIS EXERCISES
Middle-Level Thought Activities

1. Answers will vary, depending on what each student collects for the diagnostic kit. The questions should reflect the careful wording seen throughout the examples in the chapter and in the Baratta-Lorton model on text page 194.
2. This situation describes the beginning attempt at rational counting which switches back to rote counting as the numbers become larger. Answers will vary, depending on the techniques chosen by the college student. Each technique should be reasonable based on the suggestions given within the chapter.

C. SYNTHESIS and EVALUATION EXERCISES
High-Level Thought Activities

1. } Answers will vary, depending on the activities chosen.
2. Students should search professional journals for current articles on these topics, as well as "surf the net" for ideas and activities.

CHAPTER 8

EXTENDED ACTIVITY ANSWERS

ACTIVITY -- -- Different Numeration Systems

Name of the Numeration System Seen Below: Roman
    LXVII = 67   CLII = 152

Name of the Numeration System Seen Below: Mayan
    ⁑ = 12   ⁗ = 19

ACTIVITY -- -- Origin of Numerals

No answers are required here.

ACTIVITY -- -- Quipu Knots

Answers will vary.

VIDEO VIGNETTE -- Modeling Three-Digit Numbers

This vignette is movie clip 2.

In the classroom sequence, Mrs. Payne invites the children's suggestions for numbers they would like to model with the base ten blocks, and gives three examples of her own, all of which involve zero as a placeholder in the ones, tens, or tens and ones positions. (Some students may notice that Mrs. Payne says "three hundred and ninety" for her final number ... evidence that the best of us will slip up from time to time.) Students were working independently and very quickly (indeed they were praised for working fast). There was little evidence that the children were associating place value with the blocks since they counted the flats, longs, and units, all as "1, 2, 3, etc." The girl modeled the numbers 607 and 100 appropriately but it's difficult to tell the level of understanding about zero as a placeholder in this short segment. The concrete and symbolic levels are incorporated in this lesson.

Students responses to the next instructional steps will vary but should be in keeping with their analysis of the children's understanding, the philosophy of this chapter and of the NCTM Standards.

ACTIVITY -- Drawing Base Configurations

The activity shows the regroupings to be drawn from the fifth to the tenth regrouping or from the FLAT BLOCK to the FLAT BLOCK BLOCK BLOCK period.

The names of each period and its regrouping (power) are shown below from right to left as they appear in the place value system:

Power	n^{10}	n^9	n^8	n^7	n^6	n^5
Symbol	FBBB	BBB	FBB	LBB	BB	FB
Period Name	Flat Block Block Block	Block Block Block	Flat Block Block	Long Block Block	Block Block	Flat Block

Students are able to come up with the names of each generic period because they discern the pattern in each set of configurations.

ACTIVITY -- Scales of Notation

quaternary: 1 2 3 10 11 12 13 20 21 22 23 30 31 32 33 100 101 102 103 110
octary: 1 2 3 4 5 6 7 10 11 12 13 14 15 16 17 20 21 22 23 24
senary: 1 2 3 4 5 10 11 12 13 14 15 20 21 22 23 24 25 30 31 32
ternary: 1 2 10 11 12 20 21 22 100 101 102 110 111 112 120 121 122 200 201 202
nonary: 1 2 3 4 5 6 7 8 10 11 12 13 14 15 16 17 18 20 21 22
undenary: 1 2 3 4 5 6 7 8 9 A 10 11 12 13 14 15 16 17 18 19
septenary: 1 2 3 4 5 6 10 11 12 13 14 15 16 20 21 22 23 24 25 26
binary: 1 10 11 100 101 110 111 1000 1001 1010 1011 1100 1101 1110 1111 10000 10001 10010 10011

The student can use the ternary scale above as a guide in sketching the base 3 numeration system to the third regrouping.

VIDEO VIGNETTE -- Race to a Cube

This vignette is movie clip 8. The opening sequence is Dr. Mary Hatfield demonstrating the activity about to be seen in the classroom for her methods students.

In the classroom sequence, the girl on the right, in the light pink shirt, doesn't seem to recognize or understand the 10-1 relationship. She counts more than 10 longs without indicating that a trade needs to be made. The girl on the left, in the darker pink shirt, appears to count one of the units as "10" but did know that "10" meant it was time to trade, and then announced "We won." There was little discourse about the concept of place value ... it centered more upon what to do when there didn't seem to be another flat (hundreds) to trade the ten longs for.

Student responses to the student-student discourse observed, the analysis in terms of the teaching standards, and the next instructional steps will vary. Among the teaching standards that would most likely be included in the analysis would be at least one of the following: worthwhile mathematical tasks (#1), students' role in discourse (#3), tools for enhancing discourse (#4), and the learning environment (#5).

ACTIVITY -- Name the Operation

This activity is self-explanatory.

ACTIVITY -- Who Am I?

Some of the clues will have more than one answer.
21; 3; 46 or 48; 65; 99

ACTIVITY -- Number Tile Activities

This activity is self-explanatory.

ACTIVITY -- 100 Chart Fun

This activity is self-explanatory.

ACTIVITY -- Remove that Digit

This activity is self-explanatory.

ACTIVITY -- Decimal War

This activity is self-explanatory.

ACTIVITY -- Decimal Monopoly

This activity is self-explanatory.

<u>ACTIVITY -- Links for Operations</u>

Answers will vary. One example of reasoning: If this is an addition problem and I follow the order of operations convention, then 16.1 / 2 is 8.05. I add that to 12.4 and get 20.9. Now I am left with 20.9 + __ = __. If the two placeholders (since they are the same shape) are meant to hold the same number, then there is no solution. If we consider that each box can be a different number, then my solutions are infinite.

<u>ACTIVITY -- -- Abacus Action</u>

Students can demonstrate these actions on an abacus.

<u>ACTIVITY -- -- Number Tiles</u>

Answers will vary. Examples of the teacher questions are given in the activity.

EXTENDED ENDING EXERCISES

A. MEMORIZATION and COMPREHENSION EXERCISES
Low-Level Thought Activities

1. Numeration system: The process of writing or stating numbers in their natural order; a way of regrouping numerals to represent numbers.
    Number system: A mathematical system consisting of a set of objects called numbers, a set of axioms (basic propositions), and operations that act o the numbers. It is a way to classify numbers, their properties, and operations that exist no matter what numeration system is used in various cultures.
2. The answer is 1.
3. One line of reasoning goes in this way: Any number to the zero power means that no regrouping has taken place. The number is still being counted as a "one" until we know where the first regrouping occurs. An informal proof for 798 to the zero power would be as follows:
$$1 = 798^1 / 798^1 = 798^{1-1} = 798^0$$

B. APPLICATION and ANALYSIS EXERCISES
    Middle-Level Thought Activities

1. All of the following numbers have been made with the Logo
    program, BASES, but students may draw their own sylized
    version of multi-base blocks as long as each unit is clearly
    showing so the base can be seen easily within the structure of the
    blocks.

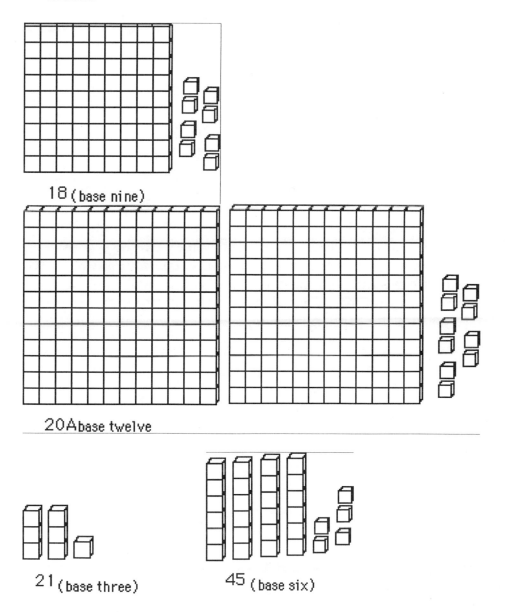

18 (base nine)

20A base twelve

21 (base three)

45 (base six)

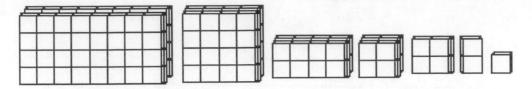

The number is 1111111_{two}

2. Answers will vary, depending on the topics and software selected.
3. Answers will vary, depending on the children's literature and topics chosen.

C. SYNTHESIS and EVALUATION EXERCISES
High-Level Thought Activities

1. The students can draw numerous chips of each color, placing them in the appropriate color categories on the chip trading mats. They they can sketch the regroupings as the chips would be in basee four and base fourteen. They may need to create more colors for the mats as the place value columns grow larger.
2. This exercise is similar to the one in the text, page 228, C-3.
3. This activity provides an excellent opportunity to search on-line databases and the NASA web-site, as well as various education sites.

CHAPTER 9

EXTENDED ACTIVITY ANSWERS

ACTIVITY -- -- Where in the World?

This activity is self-explanatory.

ACTIVITY -- -- Rummy Equations

This activity is self-explanatory.

ACTIVITY -- -- Contig

This activity is self-explanatory.

VIDEO VIGNETTE -- Concept of Ten: Fact Strategies

In the classroom sequence, the boy and girl announce the numbers spun to one another occasionally (the girl more frequently than the boy). Towards the end, the boy announces, "I need one more." The girl responds , "So do I," and then the boy says, "I win already."

Students analysis of the student-student discourse and the "worthwhileness" of the mathematical task should lead them to valuable discourse among themselves.

ACTIVITY-- -- Division by 1

4; 641; 280; 31
(The only calculators I had at hand were a TI-80 and a TI-12 [Math Explorer], which gave the expected answers.)

ACTIVITY -- Division as Repeated Subtraction

The related division equation is: $32 \div 4 = 8$

Others are:
$$56 \div 7 = 8$$
$$18 \div 2 = 9$$
$$30 \div 5 = 6$$

Each number in the equation stands for one of the following underlined parts of the question, "<u>How many groups</u> of <u>a given number</u> are in the <u>original amount (56, 18, 30)</u>?"

<u>ACTIVITY -- -- Oral Language Development</u>

Examples are given within the activity.

<u>ACTIVITY -- -- Records and Tapes of Music with the Basic</u>

The activity is self-explanatory.

<u>ACTIVITY -- -- Family Game</u>

The activity is self-explanatory.

<u>ACTIVITY -- -- Facts in Color</u>

The activity is self-explanatory.

<u>ACTIVITY -- -- Calculator Capers</u>

Target number 250 --   249 + 1 (fewest steps -- there are many ways to do this ... e.g., 248 + 2; 261-11)

Target number 63 --   3 + + = = etc. (may vary depending on the brand/model of calculator being used)

EXTENDED EXERCISES

<u>A. MEMORIZATION and COMPREHENSION EXERCISES</u>
<u>Low-Level Thought Activities</u>

1. Answer: 3
2. The counting-on strategy is used when one addend is 1, 2, or 3 beyond any given number. Therefore, 5 + 4 is NOT a good example because neither addend is 1, 2, or 3 beyond the other addend [i.e., if you start counting on with 5, you must keep track of 4 counts; if you start counting on with 4, you must keep track of 5 counts].

3. Answer: small factors or 2, 3, 4, 5 as factors.
4. An example appears on text page for the commutative property of addition. The associative property of addition, and both properties for multiplication would appear in a similar manner.
5. Sketches will vary, depending on the two Cuisenaire rods chosen.

B. APPLICATION and ANALYSIS EXERCISES
Middle-Level Thought Activities

All the answers in this section will vary, depending on the software, journals, and/or grade level chosen by the student.

C. SYNTHESIS and EVALUATION EXERCISES
High-Level Thought Activities

1. Directions for creating spreadsheets can be found in the user's manual of whatever software application is being used.
3. Answers will vary, depending on the position taken by the student.
4. A plan of remediation will vary, depending on each student's view of the problem (i.e., whether it is basic facts in addition and subtraction or multiplication and/or division). The plan should be considered a good one if the student's justifications, choice of materials, and strategies are reasonable and practical in a real classroom setting.
5. Answers will vary, but the basic strategies should follow those outlined in this chapter. Remembering their own school days, some students may suggest the game "Around the World." This would not be an efficient and meaningful way to teach the basic facts. That game is not useful until students have in fact memorized the facts and the purpose of the game is to build speed in recall.

CHAPTER 10

EXTENDED ACTIVITY ANSWERS

Video Vignette -- -- Regrouping with Addition and Base 10 Blocks

This vignette is movie clip 10.

Students will notice a number of different things in this segment, any of which can lead to an interesting discussion of "traditional" vs "standards-based" teaching. Among the points students might use as a basis for their reflection are -- The class is using manipulatives, but there does not appear to be any "real world connection" -- an abstract addition problem seems to have been posed. A context or a purpose for doing this algorithm seems to be missing. Students are using manipulatives and paper/pencil simultaneously, but it's not clear the students are making a connection between the concrete actions and the symbolic recording. One student says to "carry the one" in response to the teacher's question; the teacher replies "exchange for a ten." The teacher's request to "count the 10s" gets two different responses -- "1, 2, 3, ..." and "10, 20, 30, ..."

ACTIVITY -- -- Alternative Algorithms

This activity is self-explanatory.

ACTIVITY -- -- Napier's Bones

This activity is self-explanatory.

ACTIVITY -- -- Palindrome Pals

There are two ways to look at the first problem -- Find all of the palindromes between 50 and 150. The first is to follow the directions in the opening paragraph --

50 + 05 = 55	60 + 06 = 66
51 + 15 = 66	61 + 16 = 77
52 + 25 = 77 etc.	62 + 26 = 88 etc.

The second is simply to list all of the palindromes -- 55, 66, 77, 88, 99, 101, 111, 121, 131, 141.

If you consider only years A.D., the palindromic years are 11, 22, 33, etc. to 1991. The next palindromic year is 2002.

Answers will vary.

ACTIVITY -- -- Eye Openers

This activity is self-explanatory.

Video Vignette -- -- Dividing with Base 10 Blocks

This vignette is movie clip 10a.

The students are finding the how many of the total (37) can be shared evenly in 3 groups. This is an example of the partitive interpretation of division.

Student answers will vary, but should be consistent with the philosophy of the chapter and the NCTM standards. In a short clip like this, students may see this segment from different points. The lesson plan developed and the reflective analysis should be consistent with the objective/purpose identified by the student.

ACTIVITY -- -- Find the Largest and Smallest Answers

This activity is similar to the Missing Numbers Activity on text pages 289-290.

This can be a problem solving activity without use of a die. Or, a die can be used, and whatever number the student rolls, it is placed in one of the boxes (and cannot be subsequently moved).

ACTIVITY -- -- Creating Your Own Problems

This activity is self-explanatory.

ACTIVITY -- -- Problem Solving with a Spreadsheet

2. The formulas for filling in the remaining six cells in step 2 are:

	B	C	D
4	+A4+B1	+A4+C1	+A4+D1
5	+A5+B1	+A5+C1	+A5+D1

The values for the six cells above are:

	B	C	D
4	4903	4930	5200
5	49003	49030	49300

4. The formulas and values that should appear in column E are:

   E
1. 3000
2. +A2+E1 -- yields --> 3049
3. +A3+E1 -- yields --> 3490
4. +A4+E1 -- yields --> 7900
5. +A5+E1 -- yields --> 52000

5. An example could be:
   Change the top row to: 5   50   500   5000
   Change the side column to : 75   750   7500   75000

   NOTICE: The magnitude (number of zeros in the place value position) is the same for all numbers as it was in the original spreadsheet example.

6. One example could be to change the magnitude to:

Top row:	50000	500000	500000
Side column:	750000	7500000	75000000

   One prediction should have been that the numbers in the answer would be enlarged in proportion to the number of zeros added in each set of numbers.

be: When changing the value cells, the first formula in B2 would

For multiplication	+A2*B1
For subtraction	+A2-B1
For division	+A2/B1

1. TRY THE ALTERNATE APPROACH..

   Please note: There is an error in the text in cell D2; it should be 538. The students should be able to see the error as insufficient information and deduce that an error exists because all the other numbers fit perfectly in the addition spreadsheet.

The missing numerals would be:

	A	B	C	D
1.	Number	5	50	500
2.	38			
3.	380			
4.	3800			
5.	38000			

EXTENDED EXERCISES

A. MEMORIZATION and COMPREHENSION EXERCISES
Low-Level Thought Activities

1. The key thought is that computer spreadsheet programs can help children see the patterns involved when solving multi-digit algorithms. By carefully structuring the examples by ones, tens, hundreds, thousands, etc., the children can see the relationship of the answers to the place value of the numbers in the original problem.
2. Answers will vary, depending on the examples chosen by the students. The explanation and examples should agree with those given on text pages 272, 273, 274, and 275.

B. APPLICATION and ANALYSIS EXERCISES
Middle-Level Thought Activities

1-2. Answers will vary, depending on the student's individual choices of materials and journals.

C. SYNTHESIS and EVALUATION EXERCISES
High-Level Thought Activities

The following movements represent the regrouping of chips in the two bases:

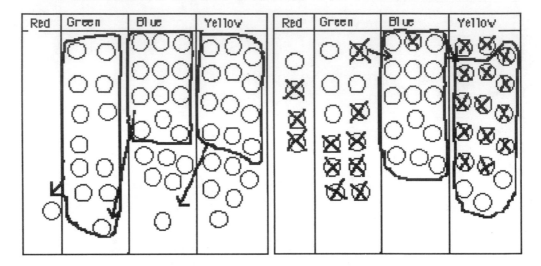

Base twelve: 76A + 4B8 = 1066   Base Fifteen: 4C02 - 370E = 14E3

You will probably recognize the two samples of children's work from the text. They are not part of the extended activities. They seem to have made their way inadvertently onto the CD-ROM.

2-3. Answers will vary.
4-5. Answers will vary, but the evaluation and justification should be in keeping with the philosophy expressed in the Standards and throughout this text.

CHAPTER 11

EXTENDED ACTIVITY ANSWERS

<u>Video Vignette -- -- Explorations with Geoboard Fractions</u>

Although we have seen other segments where the teacher speaks Spanish for the benefit of a student, this one is most interesting for the amount of Spanish used. When the instruction is in Spanish, the young girl seems to understand the concept and demonstrates her understanding. (On a personal note, I think this is an excellent argument for bilingual instruction.)

Answers will vary. Students should note the young children's struggle to conserve area ... that when the square is cut in half, and the 3 pieces are used to cover the larger triangle, the triangle has an area of only 2 squares. This is apparent also with their difficulty in grasping that 1 + 1/2 + 1/2 when seen as a square plus a triangle plus a triangle is 2 and not 3. Although a number of standards could be discussed here, students will most likely focus on Worthwhile Mathematical Tasks (#1), Tools for Enhancing Discourse (#4), and Learning Environment (#5).

<u>ACTIVITY -- -- Build a Fraction and Build a Fraction 2</u>

These activities are self explanatory.

<u>ACTIVITY -- -- Fracdecent</u>

This activity is self explanatory.

<u>ACTIVITY -- -- Target One</u>

This activity is self explanatory.

<u>ACTIVITY -- -- Working with Mixed Numbers to Fractional Numbers</u>

The materials are modeled and explained within the activity itself.

ACTIVITY -- -- Changing Fractional Numbers to Mixed Numbers

The materials are modeled and explained within the activity itself.

ACTIVITY -- -- Freaky Fractions

This activity is self explanatory.

ACTIVITY -- -- Fractimal Concentration

This activity is self explanatory.

ACTIVITY -- -- Decimal Fishing

This activity is self explanatory.

LOGO ACTIVITY -- -- Equivalent Fractions

The missing information to be typed in the equivalent fraction program is:

IF :A * :D = :B * :C [PR [THE FRACTIONS ARE EQUIVALENT.]]

LOGO ACTIVITY -- -- TrueFractions

Steps 1 and 2 are self-explanatory.

3. The following Logo drawings are made with their respective commands:

BOX1   BOX2   BOX3   REC3A

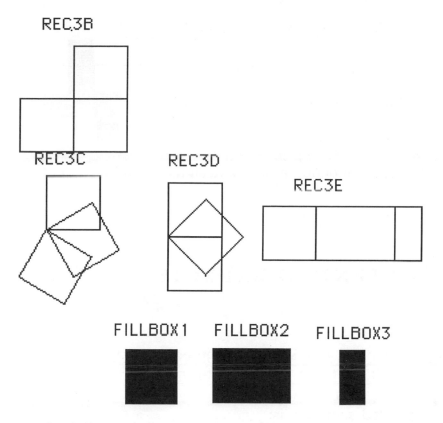

REC3B

REC3C   REC3D

REC3E

FILLBOX1   FILLBOX2   FILLBOX3

4. The following procedures represent figures where one-fourth is seen:

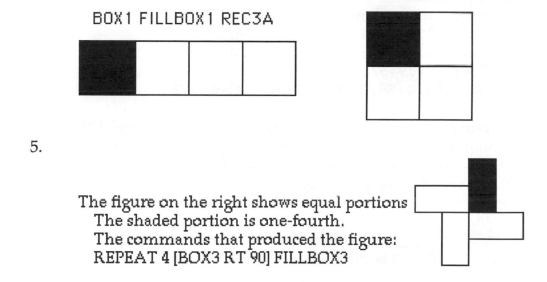

BOX1 FILLBOX1 REC3B

BOX1 FILLBOX1 REC3A

5.

The figure on the right shows equal portions
    The shaded portion is one-fourth.
    The commands that produced the figure:
    REPEAT 4 [BOX3 RT 90] FILLBOX3

6.

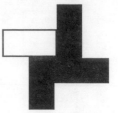

The following procedure made the figure
at the right:
REPEAT 3 [FILLBOX3 RT 90 BK 20] BOX3

7. Answers will vary, depending on the designs made by students.

EXTENDED EXERCISES

A. MEMORIZATION and COMPREHENSION EXERCISES
Low-Level Thought Activities

1. The recommended sequence is:
    a. Whole-to-part activities
    b. Partitioning representations
    c. Equivalence
    d. Operations
2. The estimation follows:
    a. Round 2 3/5÷3/4   to   3÷1   About 3
    b. Round 1 3/8÷1/3   to   1÷1/3 About 3
    c. Round 5 7/9÷5/8   to   6÷1   About 6
    d. Round 3/4÷7 1/2   to   1÷8   About 1/8

3. One-third as a repeating decimal is shown on text page 329.
    Compare that drawing to the one on the next page which shows
    0.333. notice the arrow shows the line exactly on 0.3, 0.33, and
    0.333; whereas the picture on text page 330 shows the line slightly
    to the right, indicating one-third more of the next unit. This
    holds true for the number 0.3333 as well. Therefore,

    $\overline{0.3333}$ is more

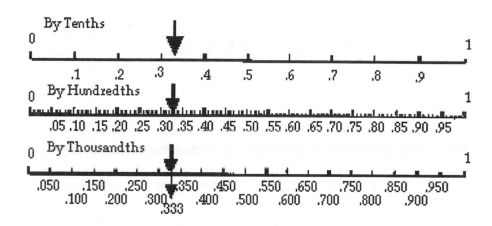

B. APPLICATION and ANALYSIS EXERCISES
Middle-Level Thought Activities

1. The computer line (of LOGO code) completes the formula for finding equivalent fractions, the ratio definition of fractions.
2. The instructor may have students build a bibliography, or if assigning exercises from part C, use these articles in the evaluation and essay.

C. SYNTHESIS and EVALUATION EXERCISES
High-Level Thought Activities

1. Answers will vary, depending upon the software selected.
2. Students should be able to summarize their position using the philosophy expressed within the chapter.
3. Answers will vary depending upon the replacement units selected.

CHAPTER 12

EXTENDED ACTIVITY ANSWERS

ACTIVITY -- -- Consumer Math

1-4. Answers will vary depending on the grocery or business ads found.
5. The directions below depend on the type of calculator being used. Consult the operating directions for your calculator. Adjustments to the following procedures may be needed.

To Find the Sale Price
a. Enter the original price and press M+ (if calculator has this key).
b. Enter original price times (x) percent of discount (as a whole number).
c. Press % key.
d. Press the minus (-) key.
e. Press M+ key.
f. The answer will be the price after the discount.

To Find the Discount Price
a. Enter the original price minus (-) the sale price equals (=)
b. The answer will be the amount reduced.
c. Then press the division key (--) and enter the original price equals (=)
d. The answer will be the decimal equivalent of the percent discounted.

To Find Commissions and the Selling Price
a. Enter the original price times (x) the percent of commission wanted (as a whole number).
b. Press the % key equals (=)
c. The answer will be the amount of the commission.
d. Press the plus key (+) and enter the original price equals (=)
e. The answer will be the selling price as the amount to charge so the commission will be paid over and above the original cost.

To Find the Percent Increase

(Found the same way as one finds the discount.)

a. The asking price is the same as the original price in the discount example.

b. The price before it was inflated to account for the increase is the same as the sale price in the discount example.

To Find the Percent Decrease

(Found the same way as one finds the discount because a discount may be defined as the percent decreased from the original price to the sale price.)

ACTIVITY -- -- Percentages in Sports

Marksmen	Total Shots	Shots Hitting Target	Percent Hitting
1	600	475	79
2	500	375	75
3	200	105	53
4	150	75	50
5	50	31	62
6	75	52	69
7	30	20	67
8	960	777	81
9	280	213	76
10	25	5	20
11	5	2	40
12	140	78	56
13	750	702	94
14	650	602	93
15	750	435	58
a) The winner:	13	best percent is:	94
b) Second place	14		
c) Last place:	10		

ACTIVITY -- -- Proportion with Real World Problems

Steps 1 and 2 are self-explanatory.

3. The proportion presented two ways:

$$\frac{3}{\$1.50} \qquad \frac{27}{\$\ X} \qquad\qquad \frac{\$1.50}{\$\ X} \qquad \frac{3}{27}$$

$$3X = \$40.50 \qquad\qquad 3X = \$40.50$$
$$X = \$13.50 \qquad\qquad X = \$13.50$$

4. The proportion presented two ways:

$$\frac{30\ feet}{60\ feet} \qquad \frac{X\ min}{3\ min} \qquad\qquad \frac{3\ min}{60\ feet} \qquad \frac{X\ min}{30\ feet}$$

$$60X = 90 \qquad\qquad 60X = 90$$
$$X = 1.5\ minutes \qquad\qquad X = 1.5\ minutes$$

Therefore, half the feet = half the time.

ACTIVITY -- -- Proportions in Economics

Step 1 is self-explanatory.

2. The following table shows the estimate and actual better buy:

Estimate	* = Better Buy	Calculator Check
2 : 1.60	* (equal value)	2/1.59 as 3/2.39
3 : 2.40	* (equal value)	$0.79 = $0.79
32 : 1.80	*	32/1.79 as 24/1.59
24 : 1.60		$0.06 = $0.07
50 : 2.00	*	50/1.99 A 32/1.69
32 : 1.70		$0.04 = $0.05

3. Answers will vary depending on the examples chosen.

ACTIVITY -- -- Finding the Height of the Flag Pole

Directions are given within the activity.
For example:

If the shadow of the ruler is 18 inches, and the length of the shadow of the flag pole is 24 feet, one way to set up the proportion is: 1 foot : 1.5 feet = x feet : 24 feet

ACTIVITY -- -- Rates and Proportions

1. Self-explanatory

2.
	Train 1	Train 2
hours =	1 hr. = n	1 hr. = n
miles =	120 600	105 450

n = 5 hours   n = 4.28 hours

Train 2 arrives first because it takes only 4 and a quarter hours to arrive at the destination compared with 5 hours for Train 1.

3.
	Store A	Store B
	n. = 12	n. = 4
	250 100	290 100
interest =	$30.00	$11.60

original price	$250	$290.00
interest	+ 30	+ 11.60
total payment	$280	$301.60

better buy = Store A   Money Saved
                              $301.60 - 280.00 = $21.60

SPREADSHEET ACTIVITY -- -- Ratio, Proportion, and Percent

5. Generalized Rule:
    To find percents from decimals, one multiplies by 100.
    To find percents when the common fraction is given, divide
        the numerator by the denominator and multiply by 100.
    To find decimals from percents, one divides by 100.

What follows in 6, 7, and 8 is from the LOGO activity ... Ratio.

6. The Logo procedures: The ratio is:
    1PART STAR 5 2PART HEX 7   5 : 7

The Logo procedures: The ratio is:
1PART OCT 5 2PART TRI 2   5 : 2

1PART PENT 7 2PART STAR 3

7. Answers will vary.
8. Step 8 is self-explanatory.

LOGO ACTIVITY -- -- Percent Pictures

Step 1 is self-explanatory.

2. The following procedures produce the Logo pictures shown:
    33%CIRCLE   75%CIRCLE   25%CIRCLE

3. To test the percentages:
    33%CIRCLE   25%CIRCLE
    33%CIRCLE   25%CIRCLE
    33%CIRCLE   25%CIRCLE
                                          25%CIRCLE

    Please Note: One cannot combine different percentages such as:
            75%CIRCLE   25%CIRCLE
    The circumferences are computed based on the first decimal in
    each procedure. Combining the procedures does not produce a
    congruent shape with the same circumference.

4. Self-explanatory
5. Self explanatory

LOGO ACTIVITY -- -- Sale Price

1. Self-explanatory
2. Self-explanatory
3. The calculator steps are exactly like those outlined in the consumer math activity.
4. For Those Who Like a Challenge:
   The following changes should have been made:
   TO PERCENTSAVED
   CLEARTEXT
   TEXTSCREEN
   PR [WHAT IS THE ORIGINAL PRICE?]
   MAKE "P FIRST READLIST
   PR [WHAT IS THE SALE PRICE?]
   MAKE "S FIRST READLIST
   MAKE "R :S / :P * 100
   MAKE "X "100 - :R
   PR [THE PERCENT SAVED IS]
   PR :X

EXTENDED EXERCISES

A. MEMORIZATION and COMPREHENSION EXERCISES
Low-Level Thought Activities

1. Answers may vary, but responses similar to the examples given on text page 353 are acceptable.
2. Answers may vary, depending on the examples chosen, but the relationships expressed should be in keeping with the information on text pages 348, 352-3, 356, and 360.
3. Answers will vary depending on the application chosen.
4. x m : 60 m = 1 m : .35 m   .35x = 60   x = 171.42857143 or 171.43 m
6. The missing numbers on the chart should be:
   0.02 x 0.2   3   0.004
   0.02 x 0.02   4   0.0004
   Through mental computation and knowing the rules of the decimal system, one can figure the answer to this equation:
   0.00000003 x 0.000003 = 0.00000000000009

B. APPLICATION and ANALYSIS EXERCISES
       Middle-Level Thought Activities

1. Hibernation
   Raindrop
   Cool
2. Answers will vary depending on the textbooks chosen.
3. Answers will vary but could include reference to scale drawings, similar figures, "better buy" comparison, etc.
4. The Logo program line supports the ratio definition of rational numbers.
5-7. Note to the instructor: #7 should read, "mathematical connections."
   Answers will vary depending upon journal articles, software, and children's literature selected.
8. Answers will vary, but stress should be on support of the philosophy of the chapter and the NCTM standards.

C. SYNTHESIS and EVALUATION EXERCISES
       High-Level Thought Activities

1. Answers will vary, depending on the lesson concept chosen.
2. Answers will vary but students should be able to give clear reasons for the similarities they describe.
3. Answers will vary, depending on the lesson concept chosen.
4. The spreadsheet documentation which accompanies all computer spreadsheet programs should help the college student to set up a spreadsheet like the one shown in this exercise.

CHAPTER 13

EXTENDED ACTIVITY ANSWERS

ACTIVITY -- -- Multiplication with Odd and Even Numbers

The "previous calculator exploration" refers to the activity in the text, page 372 ... Addition with Odd and Even Numbers.

Examples will vary, but the rule will remain constant.

Even x Even:	Odd x Odd:	Even x Odd:
10 x 4 = 40	3 x 7 = 21	6 x 7 = 42
908 x 22 = 19976	751 x 95 = 71345	836 x 59 = 49324
Rule:	Rule:	Rule:
When 2 even numbers are multiplied, the result will be	When 2 odd numbers are multiplied, the result will be	When an odd and an even number are multiplied, the result will be
even	even	odd

ACTIVITY -- -- Odd and Even Numbers

Examples will vary, but the following observations should be made:

Even + Even + Even = Even   Odd + Odd + Even + Even = Even
Even + Odd + Odd = Even   Odd x Odd x Odd = Odd

ACTIVITY -- -- Large Numbers with the Sieve of Eratosthenes

Steps 1 and 2 are explained within the activity. (The procedure for the number 201 can be found on text page 374. It can also be found in the activity on the CD-ROM, "Finding Prime Numbers Like the Ancient Ones Did.")
3. The following numbers are squared:
   33 = 1089
   34 = 1156
   35 = 1225
   36 = 1296
   37 = 1369 ---> Therefore, the primes we will look at will be at

38 = 1444 ---> or below 37, looking at the Sieve we find these
easily:
37, 31, 29, 19, 17, 13, 11, 7, 5, 3, 2

4. Using the primes listed above, we will look for one of them to divide evenly into the number, 1373; thereby making it a composite number. If no composite number can be found, then the number can be declared a prime.

5.

Divisible by:	Answer:	Is this a composite number?
1373 / 37 =	37.10	No
1373 / 31 =	44.29	No
1373 / 29 =	47.34	No
1373 / 23 =	59.69	No
1373 / 19 =	72.26	No
1373 / 17 =	80.76	No
1373 / 13 =	105.61	No
1373 / 11 =	124.81	No
1373 / 7 =	196.14	No
1373 / 5 =	274.60	No
1373 / 3 =	457.66	No
1373 / 2 =	686.50	No

Therefore, 1373 can be divided only by itself and 1; so it is a PRIME number.

ACTIVITY -- -- Finding Prime Numbers Like the Ancient Ones Did

This activity is self-explanatory.

ACTIVITY -- -- Divisibility by 3 and 9: Explaining the Rule

The activity is self explanatory.

ACTIVITY -- -- Pascal's Triangle
1.

level 7	1 7 21 35 35 21 7 1	128
level 8	1 8 28 56 70 56 28 8 1	256
level 9	1 9 36 84 126 126 84 36 9 1	512

2. Answers will vary as students observe different patterns within the triangle.

ACTIVITY -- -- Simultaneous Equations from China

The activity is self explanatory.

LOGO ACTIVITY -- -- Perfect Squares

The Chart:

Square #	Side	Area
Square 1	1	1
Square 2	2	4
Square 3	3	9
Square 4	4	16
Square 5	5	25
Square 6	6	36
Square 7	7	49
Square 8	8	64
Square 9	9	81
Square 10	10	100
Predict		
Square 11	11	121
Square 12	12	144

LOGO ACTIVITY -- -- Figurate Numbers

CAUTION STUDENTS to use the PENUP command to move the turtle to the lower left portion of the screen to start a figure.

REMEMBER, use the PENDOWN command before drawing the figure.

Steps 1 through 5 are self-explanatory.

6. For a heptagonal number   For an octagonal number
    FIG 7 6   FIG 8 6

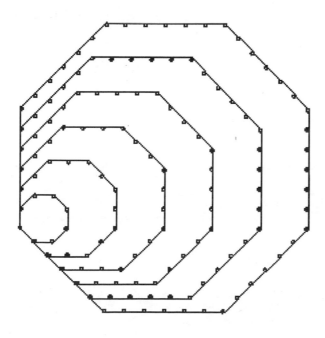

For a nonagonal number
FIG 9 6

The Hexagonal figure in Figure 12.4 and the subsequent number pattern:

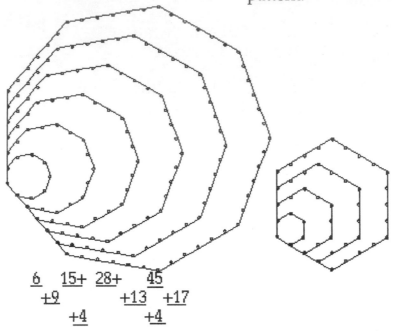

$$\underline{6} \quad \underline{15+} \quad \underline{28+} \quad \underline{45}$$
$$\underline{+9} \qquad \underline{+13} \; \underline{+17}$$
$$\underline{+4} \qquad \underline{+4}$$

LOGO ACTIVITY -- -- Fibonacci

The program commands on the left will yield the printout on the right:

```
TO FIBONACCI
TEXTSCREEN                              FIBONACCI
PR [THIS PROGRAM PRINTS]        THIS PROGRAM PRINTS
PR [FIBONACCI NUMBERS]          FIBONACCI NUMBERS
PR [TO LEVEL 14.]                    TO LEVEL 14.
MAKE "N  "0                          LEVEL 1 = 1
MAKE "A  "1                          LEVEL 2 = 1
MAKE "B  "1                          LEVEL 3 = 2
MAKE "C  "1                          LEVEL 4 = 3
FIBFORMULA                           LEVEL 5 = 5
                                     LEVEL 6 = 8
TO FIBFORMULA                        LEVEL 7 = 13
MAKE "N  :N + 1                      LEVEL 8 = 21
IF  :N < 3 [MAKE "C  "1]             LEVEL 9 = 34
IF  :N = 15 [STOP]                   LEVEL 10 = 55
TYPE "LEVEL TYPE  :N TYPE "= TYPE  :C LEVEL 11 = 89
PR [ ]                               LEVEL 12 = 144
MAKE "A  :B                          LEVEL 13 = 233
MAKE "B  :C                          LEVEL 14 = 377
MAKE "C  :A  +  :B
FIBFORMULA
END
```

EXTENDED EXERCISES

A. MEMORIZATION and COMPREHENSION EXERCISES
Low-Level Thought Activities

1. The difference between prime and composite numbers may be
   seen in the number of factors that can be generated by each set.
   A prime number can have <u>only</u> two factors -- itself and one. The
   Cuisenaire rods on this and the next page show several prime
   numbers on the left and composite numbers on the right.
   Notice the evidence of multiple factors show in the composite
   numbers.

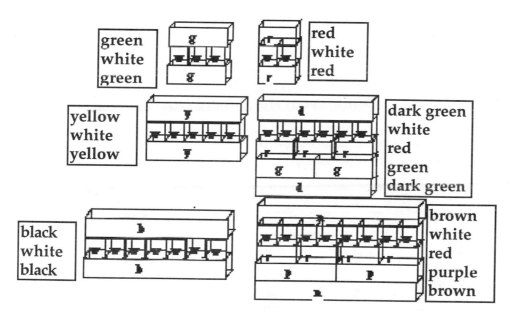

2. The rules are first modeled by disks and then by graph paper.
   Each involves the idea of "pairing" objects. If all the objects can
   be paired, then the numbers are even.

Even + Even	Odd + Odd	Even + Odd
2 + 4	3 + 5	2 + 3

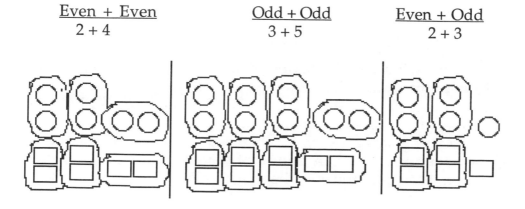

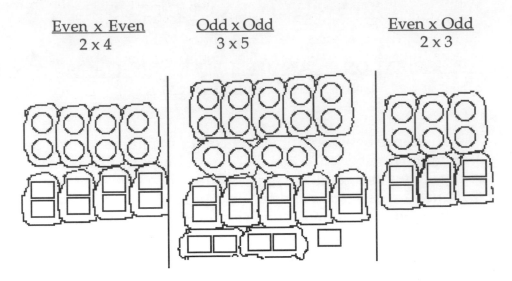

Even x Even   Odd x Odd   Even x Odd
2 x 4   3 x 5   2 x 3

3. Answers will vary, depending on the students' own words and the examples they choose.

B. APPLICATION and ANALYSIS EXERCISES
     Middle-Level Thought Activities

1. Prime towers with Cuisenaire rods . . .
   Number 8   Number 6   Number 12

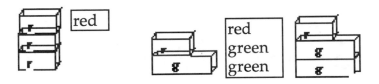

The LCM is the most of any color that any tower uses.
          3 red rods and 1 green rod
          2 x 2 x 2 x 3 = 24

The GCF is the color that is in common in all three towers.
          The red rod or 2

Yes, the LCM and GCF were the same in the concrete and symbolic methods.

2. Answers will vary, depending on the two numbers chosen.

3. Note to the instructor: This exercise is from the second edition and was inadvertently left in this third edition. If you have used this text in its earlier editions, you will have noted that the BASIC programs have been eliminated in favor of LOGO. If you have the second edition, and want to look up the program and assign it to your students, the answer follows.

Using the Sieve of Eratosthenes, primes beyond those seen in the BASIC program in lines 70 to 160 can be added to test larger numbers. Those primes are seen in lines 170 to 185. The original line 180 becomes 186. The beginning part of the program needs to be changed to reflect the check for numbers between 1600 and 9404. Since 9404 is 97 x 97 (the last prime to be checked in the new program), the new BASIC program will test numbers as high as 9404.

```
20 PRINT "TYPE IN A NUMBER FROM 1600 TO 9409."
50 PRINT IF A < 1600 THEN 300
60 PRINT IF A > 9404 THEN 340
170 PRINT A; "/31 IS "; A/31
171 PRINT A; "/37 IS "; A/37
172 PRINT A; "/41 IS "; A/41
173 PRINT A; "/43 IS "; A/43
174 PRINT A; "/47 IS "; A/47
175 PRINT A; "/53 IS "; A/53
176 PRINT A; "/59 IS "; A/59
178 PRINT A; "/61 IS "; A/61
179 PRINT A; "/67 IS "; A/67
180 PRINT A; "/71 IS "; A/71
181 PRINT A; "/73 IS "; A/73
182 PRINT A; "/79 IS "; A/79
183 PRINT A; "/83 IS "; A/83
184 PRINT A; "/89 IS "; A/89
185 PRINT A; "/97 IS "; A/97
186 PRINT "LOOK AT THE LIST ABOVE."
320 PRINT "THAN 1600.  TRY AGAIN."
360 PRINT "THAN 9404.  TRY AGAIN."
```

4. Answers will vary, depending on the numbers chosen.
8. Answers will vary, depending on the computer programs reviewed.

C. SYNTHESIS and EVALUATION EXERCISES
High-Level Thought Activities

1. Primes = 1, 10, 11, 101, 111, 1011, 1101 in base two.
2. All bases will have divisibility rules; the difference is that they will be based on the properties of their number systems. Knowing how to find the divisibility rules in our base ten system should help us know how to evaluate the rules in other bases.
3. The students' programs will be similar to the following:

```
TO FIBONACCI
PR [THIS PROGRAM PRINTS]
PR [FIBONACCI NUMBERS]
PR [TO LEVEL 14.]
MAKE "N  "0
MAKE "A  "1
MAKE "B  "1
MAKE "C  "1
FIBFORMULA

TO FIBFORMULA
MAKE "N  :N + 1
IF :N < 3 [MAKE "C  "1]
IF :N = 15 [STOP]
PR [LEVEL]
INSERT :N PR [ = ] TAB INSERT :C
PR []
MAKE "A  :B
MAKE "B  :C
MAKE "C  :A + :B
FIBFORMULA
END
```

4. Answers will vary, depending on the computer topic chosen.
5. Answers will vary, depending on the students' familiarity with spreadsheets.
6. Answers will vary, depending on the functions chosen.
7. Answers will vary, but each should support the main ideas of the philosophy of the chapter.

CHAPTER 14

EXTENDED ACTIVITY ANSWERS

ACTIVITY -- -- Pictographs with Sandpaintings and Native
American Pictographs

These activities are self explanatory.

ACTIVITY -- -- Picture Graph with School-Community Activities

1. Self-explanatory
2. Row 3 contributed the most bundles. Row 4 contributed the
   least. No rows contributed the same number of bundles.
3. If each bundle pictured = 3 bundles, then:
   Row 1:   Has 12 bundles
   Row 2:   Has 9 bundles
   Row 3:   Has 18 bundles
   Row 4:   Has 6 bundles
   Row 5:   Has 15 bundles

ACTIVITY -- TEXT PAGE 757 ~~~~~~~~~~ Picture Graph

The new graph is below. The questions created by students will
vary.

ACTIVITY -- -- Bar Graphs with Favorite Sports

Answers will vary depending on the information gathered by the
class.

ACTIVITY -- -- Line Graphs

A. Message: Joy is taller than Judy, but Judy weighs more than Joy.

B. Message: Annette and Sherian are the same weight, but Sherian is taller than Annette.

C. Message: Jackie and Krista are the same weight, but Krista is taller than Jackie.

D. Message: J.C. is taller and heavier than Bob.

E. Message: Tammy and Karen are the same age, but Karen weighs less than Tammy.

F. Message: Frank is younger than Paul or Lyman, but Lyman and Paul are the same age. Paul is the shortest, followed by Frank, and Lyman is the tallest.

Describe: As time advances, speed decelerates.

Describe: As speed increases, time decelerates.

ACTIVITY -- -- Line Graphs with Speed and Time

1. Describe: As time advances, speed decelerates.

2. Describe: As speed increases, time decelerates.

A. Conclusion: Speed starts quickly, levels out over time and accelerates near the finish of a time sequence.

B. Conclusion: Speed accelerates over time, gradually leveling out as time slows to a constant rate.

C. Conclusion: Speed slows as time advances.

D. Conclusion: Speed accelerates and decelerates at an uneven pace as time continues to advance.

ACTIVITY -- -- More Practice with Messages in Line Graphs

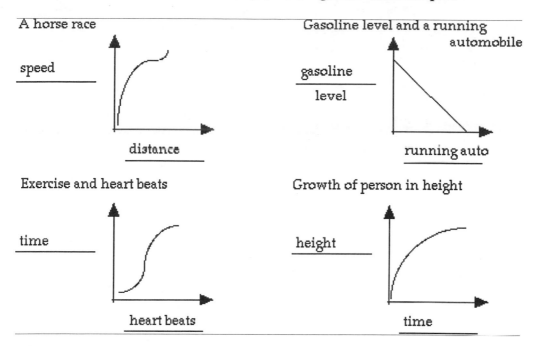

ACTIVITY -- -- Kinds of Graphs Compared

Students can be asked to identify the different types of graphs shown here. They can explain which seem to give the "best" representation of the data and the different reasons for using the different types of graphs. When might one be preferred over another?

ACTIVITY -- -- Finding the Mean: The Pictorial level

The activity is self explanatory.

ACTIVITY -- -- Finding the Mean: The Symbolic level

The averages in each cell give a magic square of the sum 355.05.

189.36	23.67	142.02
71.01	118.35	165.69
94.68	213.03	47.34

ACTIVITY -- -- Mode

The activity is self explanatory.

ACTIVITY -- -- Finding the Average in Sports

The average can be found for each league by adding the number of wins, losses and ties of each team to find its total games played. Then the number of GF and GA can be averaged per game by dividing each of them by the total games played by each team.

The bar graphs may vary, depending on the computer program chosen.

ACTIVITY -- -- Money Toss

Steps 1 through 4 are self-explanatory.
5. The probability that both coins are heads is 1/4.
6. The probability that one coin is heads and one tails is 1/2.
7. The probability that at least one coin is tails is 3/4.

ACTIVITY -- -- Creating Tables with Dice Tosses

1-2. Answers will vary, depending on the toss of the dice.
3. The following table shows the mathematical probabilities for the sums:

Sum	2	3	4	5	6	7	8	9	10	11	12
Chances	1	2	3	4	5	6	5	4	3	2	1

4. 7 occurs most often; 1 & 12 occur least often
5. Answers will vary depending on results.
6. Theoretical probabilities are not certainties; actual results can differ significantly from mathematical probabilities.

ACTIVITY -- -- Permutations with Selecting People & Other
Interesting Things

1. $3! = 3 \times 2 \times 1 = 6$
2. $3! = 3 \times 2 \times 1 = 6$
3. $_{52}P_4 = \dfrac{52!}{(52-4)!} = \dfrac{52!}{48!} = 52 \times 51 \times 50 \times 49 = 6{,}497{,}400$
4. $9! = 9 \times 8 \times 7 \times 6 \times 5 \times 4 \times 3 \times 2 \times 1 = 362{,}880$
5. $_{10}P_4 = \dfrac{10!}{(10-4)!} = \dfrac{10!}{6!} = 10 \times 9 \times 8 \times 7 = 5{,}040$

ACTIVITY -- -- Boxes of Candy

This activity is self explanatory.

ACTIVITY -- -- Combinations with Cards

1. = $\dfrac{52!}{4!\,(52-4)!}$ = $\dfrac{52!}{4!\,48!}$ = $\dfrac{52 \times 51 \times 50 \times 49}{4 \times 3 \times 2 \times 1}$ = $\dfrac{6,497,400}{24}$ = 270,725

$_{52}C_4$

2. = $\dfrac{8!}{5!\,(8-5)!}$ = $\dfrac{8!}{5!\,3!}$ = $\dfrac{8 \times 7 \times 6}{3 \times 2 \times 1}$ = $\dfrac{336}{6}$ = 56

$_{8}C_5$

3. = $\dfrac{16!}{2!\,(16-2)!}$ = $\dfrac{16!}{2!\,14!}$ = $\dfrac{16 \times 15}{2 \times 1}$ = $\dfrac{240}{2}$ = 120

$_{16}C_2$

4. = $\dfrac{14!}{4!\,(14-4)!}$ = $\dfrac{14!}{4!\,10!}$ = $\dfrac{14 \times 13 \times 12 \times 11}{4 \times 3 \times 2 \times 1}$ = $\dfrac{24024}{24}$ = 1001

$_{14}C_4$

5. = $\dfrac{7!}{4!\,(7-4)!}$ = $\dfrac{7!}{4!\,3!}$ = $\dfrac{7 \times 6 \times 5}{3 \times 2 \times 1}$ = $\dfrac{2110}{6}$ = 35

$_{7}C_4$

ACTIVITY -- -- Combinations with Cards

This activity is self-explanatory.

ACTIVITY -- -- Reading/Alphabet with Circle Graphs
Steps 1 through 5 are self-explanatory.
6. When using the circle graph, the rankings should add up to 100 percent so the portions on the circle graph clearly represent all the choices in the correct proportions.

ACTIVITY -- -- Circle Graphs

1. The answer is found within the example given.
2. The set up directions will differ, depending on the computer program chosen. If the Logo program PROTRACTOR is adapted, the following steps will need to be taken:
   a. Because the Logo procedure finds angle sizes, each percentage must be given the angle size that corresponds to each percentage:

Decimal Equivalent of the %	X 360 Degrees	Angle Size on Circle Graph
.375	X 360	135
.125	X 360	45
.20	X 360	72
.30	X 360	108
		Total = 360

b. Enter the degrees after resetting the protractor to zero each time. The angle turns to the left, adding the degrees that have gone before, and then draws the next angle:

A 135
RESET LT 135 A 45
RESET LT 180 A 72
RESET LT 252 A 108

3. Answers will vary.

ACTIVITY -- -- Comparing Different Types of Graphs

1. The answer is found within the example given.
2-3. The following bar graph shows the same information presented on two different scales and graphs.

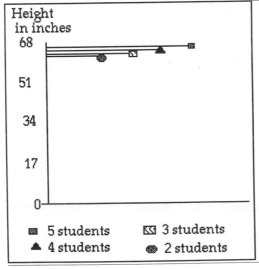

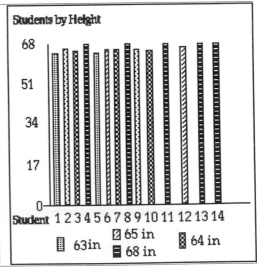

ACTIVITY -- -- SPREADSHEET

3. Type in the cell formula below to find:

	Team Total	Average / Player
Minutes	@SUM (B5.B14)	@AVG (B5.B14)
Rebounds	@SUM (G5.G14)	@AVG (G5.G14)
Assists	@SUM (H5.H14)	@AVG (H5.H14)
Totals	@SUM (J5.J14)	@AVG (J5.J14)D

4.

	Averages for Both Teams
Minutes	@AVG (B16.B32)
Rebounds	@AVG (G16.G32)
Assists	@AVG (H16.H32)
Totals	@AVG (J16.J32)D

5. The line graphs present each player's FG by team, using a computer graphing program:

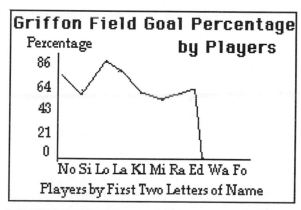

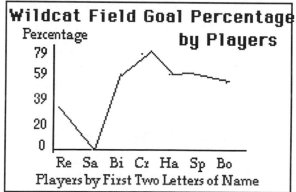

EXTENDED EXERCISES

<u>A. MEMORIZATION and COMPREHENSION EXERCISES</u>
<u>Low-Level Thought Activities</u>

1. Use any computer graphing program to complete these graphs.
2.   Round 1:   Mean = 70   Mode = 70
         Round 2:   Mean = 67.1 Mode = 67
3. Any computer graphing program can be used. The cost would be:
   $ 31,824
   $ 66,454
   $ 184,462
   $ 5,400
   $ 404,880

4. <u>Salesperson</u>   <u>% Positive Results for Contacts Made</u>
   1 Wilkerson   80
   2 Mahaffy   53
   3 Gunn   64
   4 Coyne   87
   5 Nunez   85
   6 Roever   94
   7 Murphy   65

   Average number of tickets sold per person = <u>183</u>
   Salesperson who sold most tickets = <u>Wilkerson</u>
   Salesperson who sold least tickets = <u>Mahaffy</u>
   Highest average sold per contact = <u>94% by Roever</u>
   Lowest average sold per contact = <u>53% by Mahaffy</u>
   Mean number of tickets sold per hour = <u>91.5</u>   per minute = <u>1.5</u>

5.

Range = 19 - 30
Mean = 25
Median = 24.5
Mode = 24

6-7. Answers will vary, depending upon the textbooks and software selected.

B. APPLICATION and ANALYSIS EXERCISES
Middle-Level Thought Activities

1-7. Answers will vary, depending on the topic chosen.

C. SYNTHESIS and EVALUATION EXERCISES
High-Level Thought Activities

1-13. Answers will vary, depending on the topic and the lesson chosen.

14. The Logo program, PROTRACTOR, can be modified in a number of different ways to create circle graphs.

TEST SECTION

SECTION C

For this third edition of the instructor's manual, you will notice that not all tests have 20 questions. With the emphasis on alternative or authentic assessment, it seemed incumbent upon us to provide more of that type of assessment for those who use this text. No doubt you will have samples of your own that you may wish to substitute for those provided here.

You might want to forewarn your students that some of the multiple choice items are actually multiple mark items. Almost every chapter includes one or two larger tasks, such as developing a rubric or scoring guide and critiquing student work or evaluating a lesson plan. The student work is actual student work. The lesson plans were developed by students in elementary mathematics methods.

TEST QUESTIONS --

MIDTERM/FINAL ALTERNATIVES

For the midterm or final exam, students might be asked to submit a portfolio of their best work. One approach would be to have the students organize the portfolio around characteristics of a professional educator; e.g., critical thinker, creative planner, and effective practitioner.

Each section is prefaced with a rationale, written by the student, for including the selected items in that category.

A specific number of pieces can be required, e.g, five (5) pieces of work, with at least one piece in each category. Or, a range of pieces can be assigned, e.g., 7-10 pieces, with at least two pieces in each category.

Students can select pieces from their chapter assignments, entries from their journals or logs, audio or video tapes of a "teach," photographs of a bulletin board or project, etc.

TEST QUESTIONS -- CHAPTER 1

p 13
L()   1. Some of the technology showing the most potential for helping students learn mathematics include:
    a. interactive multimedia
    b. programming in FORTRAN, COBOL and TurboC
    c. digital media
    d. Internet
    e. programming in LOGO with *Turtle Math*

p 12
M()   2. Chapter 1 suggested that renovation of the mathematics curriculum should include which of the following:
    a. curricula to develop proof and deductive reasoning
    b. curricula to build an accepted body of mathematical knowledge
    c. curricula to emphasize computational skills.
    d. curricula to increase students' abilities to apply mathematics

p 5ff
M()   3. You are teaching students in the year 2020. From the 1989 NCTM <u>Standards</u>, you can expect your students to be:
    a. communicating the results of their mathematical investigations to other students
    b. using the computer to verify mathematical investigations done by the slide rule
    c. using problem solving and higher-ordered thinking skills to memorize the 100 addition basic facts
    d. studying mathematics topics that were not part of the mathematics curriculum in 1989

p CD
M()   4. Which of the classroom scenes below support the use of calculators as reported in research findings?
    a. Students only use calculators to check their paper and pencil computations.
    b. Students are using calculators to do problem solving tasks.
    c. Students are using calculators when doing tedious computation exercises.
    d. Students are using calculators to improve the quickness of doing the basic 100 number facts.

p 13ff

H(v) 5. You have just been hired as an elementary or middle school mathematics teacher in a district that is paying attention to technological changes in the field of mathematics. You are asked to submit a list of instructional aids to be purchased for your classroom. What would be the top 3 items you would request and why?

CD

H(v) 6. The authors of your text include, on the CD-ROM several issues as factors that have affected or are affecting mathematics teaching in our schools. Select three of the issues and describe <u>how</u> each has influenced or is influencing the teaching of mathematics in elementary schools.

p 7ff
&CD

H(v) 7. Choose one of the six Standards for Teaching Mathematics from the NCTM's <u>Professional Standards for Teaching Mathematics</u>. Evaluate how the implementation of this standard will cause your classroom teaching to differ from the classroom instruction you received as an elementary school student.

p 5ff

H(v) 8. John Dewey believed that all learning should be relevant to the student's experience. Compare his philosophy with the NCTM *Curriculum Standards* and show how you would apply the idea of relevancy to the student's experience to teaching estimation, mental math, and mathematical connections. Give specific examples.

CD

H(v) 9. A number of trends in mathematics education were discussed in the CD ROM portion of Chapter 1: calculators, microcomputers, problem solving, estimation, mental math, mathematical connections, and manipulatives. Prioritize these trends, ranking them from most necessary to less necessary to be an effective citizen in the future. Justify your answer.

p 3ff
H(v) 10. Describe at least <u>two things</u> about the teaching of elementary school mathematics that has <u>changed significantly</u> over the last few decades.

CD
H(v) 11. Many parents are still highly resistant to the use of calculators in elementary school mathematics. Write a letter to the parents of your class explaining when and why you will be expecting your students to use calculators.

= Cover Up Next Portion When Copying Test =

ANSWERS TO HIGHER LEVEL QUESTIONS

L()   1. a, c, d, e

M()   2. a, c, d

M()   3. a, d

M()   4. b, c

H(v) 5. Student answers will vary . . .The college student should be able to give sufficient detail for each instructional item selected that the instructor can see the student's understanding of the purpose for which the items will be used.

H(v) 6. Student answers will vary . . . The college student should be able to give at least one example for each of the three issues in sufficient detail that the instructor can see the student understands the influence each has exerted upon the teaching of mathematics.

H(v) 7. Student answers will vary . . . The college student should be able to give sufficient detail in the evaluation that the instructor can see the student's grasp of the need for change in classroom instruction.

H(v) 8. Student answers will vary . . . The college student should be able to give at least one example for each of the three concepts in sufficient detail that the instructor can see that the math concept is relevant to children's thinking and experience in elementary or middle school.

H(v) 9. Student answers will vary . . . The order in which the
           college student places the trends is optional but the
           justification statements should explain why the first was
           considered the most important, etc. down to the last trend
           and its status as less important.

H(v) 10. Student answers will vary . . . The description should
           include those elements that indicate a significant change
           in mathematics instruction.

H(v) 11. Student answers will vary . . . The letter should state
           clearly the reasons for using calculators in the classroom.
           The reasons given should indicate the student's
           awareness of the appropriate use of calculators and should
           be in keeping with the NCTM's position on the use of
           calculators.

p 29
L(c)   1. Chapter 2 has stressed the need to use _____
        materials first when introducing any new concept in
        elementary school mathematics.
        a. iconic
        b. symbolic
        c. concrete
        d. pictorial

p 29
L()   2. Chapter 2 also stressed the need for preschool and
        elementary teachers to use these tools to stimulate brain
        development in young children.
        a. rote memorization
        b. manipulatives
        c. higher order thinking questions
        d. interactive technology

p 38
L(b)   3. Labinowicz (1985) suggests that teachers discourage
        "parroting" responses by students. Which of the
        following phrases does Labinowicz recommend teachers
        use?
        a. "Prove your answer is the correct one by doing the
           work again."
        b. "How would you explain this to a first grader who
           doesn't understand it?"
        c. "Reread the problem aloud to justify your answer."
        d. b and c

p 49
L(s)   4. According to Polya, the problem solving process involves
        four phases:

        a. _____

        b. _____

        c. _____

        d. _____

p 47ff
M()   5. Three characteristics of a good problem solver are:
a. supplies missing or implied information
b. utilizes all the numbers in the problem to arrive at an answer
c. breaks problem down into smaller units
d. observes his/her own actions and mental processes as he/she works on problems

p 42
M(b) 6. Students who are able to answer problems like example #2 but find it hard to answer problems like example #1 are experiencing _____ thought processing.

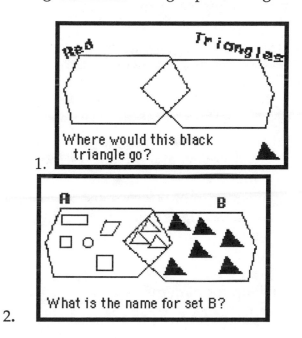

1.

2.

a. part-to-whole
b. field-dependent
c. field-independent
d. a and c

p38ff
M(d) 7. Here is a dialogue between a teacher and a student in the class:
T: Mr. Smith drives a 900 pound semi (truck) for the A-1 Trucking Company. He carries 420 pounds of office supplies to stores in the immediate area every two weeks. How many pounds of office supplies does he deliver in four weeks?

S: That's a lot of big numbers to handle. There were 900 pounds plus 420 pounds added 4 times.

T: Let's see ... we only need to know about office supplies. What sentences have the words, "office supplies", in them?

S: Sentences 2 and 3.

T: If we concentrate on the numbers in those sentences, it might give us the clues we need.

S: Okay .. that's 420 pounds for 2 weeks and 2 weeks more is 4 weeks.

T: So what happens in the last 2 weeks?

S: 420 more pounds are delivered. So that's 420 + 420 or 840 in all.

THE TEACHER IS USING:
a. the elimination of extraneous data
b. the elaborating technique
c. estimation and checking
d. a and b

p 52

M(d) 8. Analyze the problem below:

Maria was given a check from her mother which Maria cashed at the bank. She spent $5.38 for a giant can of popcorn and $0.59 for a bag of jelly beans. How much did she have left?

This is an example of:
a. Simplifying the problem
b. Working backwards
c. Looking for patterns
d. Insufficient information

p 55

M() 9. The student who answered $4.00 to the problem above could be diagnosed by the teacher as a student who
a. estimates answers.
b. looks for key words to tell which math operation should be used.
c. understands the action of the problem by modeling what is happening in the problem.
d. assumes that Maria had $10.

p 49

M(a) 10. The word problem in #7 is an example of the _____ type of question in the classification scheme presented in Chapter 2.

a. discovery
b. guided discovery
c. open-ended
d. b and c

p 56
M(c) 11. According to research by Capper (1984), a teacher who
          wants students to be successful problem solvers would use
          these words as part of the lesson:
          a. "Read the problem only once to set the situation in
              your mind."
          b. "All the information is important so use it all in the
              problem."
          c. "What was your mind thinking of as you came up with
              your solution?"
          d. "Did you write down each fact in the problem and
              work the facts from the first to the last item as they
              were presented in the problem?"

p 36
M(s) 12. Current research (Artzt and Newman, 1990) indicates that
          problem solving in cooperative groups may increase
          students' metacognitive abilities. Describe three
          behaviors that such students would exhibit.

p 48ff
M(v) 13. You are working with your students on problem solving
          strategies. How would you explain the
          idea/purpose/importance of heuristics?

p 56ff
H(v) 14. Describe two assessment techniques that you might use to
          evaluate students' progress in the use of problem solving
          strategies. Justify your choices by comparing the results
          you obtain from these techniques as compared to the
          information you would gain from a multiple choice test
          over the same material.

p 52ff
H(v) 15. Use the information in the picture below to create a word
          problem which requires simplifying the problem and
          working backwards in order to solve it. Work the
          problem and label each strategy used to arrive at the
          solution.

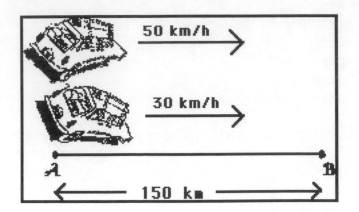

p 29ff

H(v) 16. Compare and contrast the learning theories found within the three schools of thought - Constructivist; Behaviorist; Information Processing - discussed in this chapter.

p 39ff

H(v) 17. Create two EPRs that could be used to help teach one of the problem solving strategies discussed in Chapter 2. Give an example of how each EPR will be used.

p 53

H(v) 18. Using the model of a flowchart seen in Chapter 2, create a new example of a situation that elementary or middle school children would enjoy. Ask at least three sets of Yes-No questions as a part of the flowchart.

p 44ff

H(v) 19. Describe the impact that planning for learning styles and multiple intelligences will have for children's learning of mathematics.

== Cover Up Next Portion When Copying Test ==

ANSWER TO HIGHER LEVEL QUESTIONS

L()   2. b, c, d

L(s)   4.   a. understands the question and is motivated to answer it
            b. has learned facts and strategies useful in solving problems
            c. applies various strategies until the problem is solved
            d. checks the solution to see if it is correct

M()   5. a, c, d

M()   9. a, b, d

M(s) 12. Student answers will vary . . . The behaviors described
          should be in keeping with the ideas presented on text
          pages 36 - 38.

M(v) 13. Students answers will vary . . . The student's answer
          should reflect an understanding of the use of heuristics
          and the ability to express that understanding in a way that
          is meaningful to elementary and middle school children.

H(v) 14. Student answers will vary . . . The college students should
          label points clearly so that the instructor can see the
          reasoning used.

H(v) 15. Student answers will vary, but something similar to the
          strategies below should be expected.
          The Problem
          It is 150 kilometers from point A to point B. If the car
          traveling at 50 km per hour arrives at point B at 2:00 p.m.,
          what is the starting time for the car traveling 30 km per
          hour to arrive at point B at the same time as the first car
          (2:00 p.m.)?
          Simplifying the Problem
          Let 5 stand for 50
          Let 3 stand for 30
          Let 15 stand for 150

          The first car = 5 x 3 = 15; it took 3 times to arrive at 15 so 3
          hours is the answer
          The second car = 3 x 5 = 15; it took 5 times to arrive at 15 so
          5 hours is the answer. 5 hours of traveling means the
          second car left at 9:00 a.m.
          Working Backwards
          1. We already know the distance and time of arrival for
          the first car.
          2. We will need to work backward from 2:00 p.m. to find
          the starting time of the second car.
          3. The solution is 2:00 p.m. - 5 hours = 9:00 a.m.

H(v) 16. Answers will vary depending on the strategies and
H(v) 17. problem situations chosen. The college students should
H(v) 18. label points clearly so the instructor can see the reasoning
H(v) 19. pattern clearly.

p 69
L(s)

1. Name the two facets contained within the definition of *culturally relevant mathematics*.

    a. _____

    b. _____

p 88
L(d)

2. African American and Hispanic American students are likely to score higher on standardized achievement tests if they are taught _____ procedures to approach word problems.
    a. a 3-step
    b. a 2-step
    c. writing an open sentence
    d. general

p 84
L(b)

3. Students whose predominant use of computers involves drill and practice programs would be described in the research as belonging to which class of people?
    a. those who do not have access
    b. those who have limited access
    c. those who have unlimited access
    d. those who write computer programs

p 84
L(d)

4. According to NAEP results (Mullis et al, 1991), what percentage of students had access to a personal or family calculator?
    a. 27%
    b. 44%
    c. 52%
    d. nearly 100%

p 90
L(dep)

5. A teacher with a class of predominantly Native American students would want to include a number of field _____ examples and tasks when presenting a new mathematical concept.

p 87

M(a)   6. A student who makes a "variable-reversal error" would
          choose which answer for the following problem:
          Write an equation using the variables P and T to represent
          the following statement:
          "There are 5 times as many parrots as turtles at a
          certain pet store." Use P for the number of parrots
          and T for the number of turtles.

          a. $5P = T$
          b. $5T = P$
          c. $P + T = 5$
          d. $P/T = 5$

p 84ff

M(v)   7. Compare the benefits of calculator access and use to that
          of computers for students from culturally-diverse
          backgrounds.

p. 86ff

M(v)   8. Describe two problems that LEP students may have when
          trying to solve word problems.

p. CD

M(v)   9. Describe some possible consequences that can result if we
          fail to address the issue of underrepresented groups in
          mathematics education.

p CD

M(v) 10. You are writing a grant proposal for funding for an
          innovative mathematics program. One of the
          requirements of the grant is that your program serve
          "underrepresented groups." What groups would you
          include in your grant proposal to satisfy this
          requirement?

p CD

M(v) 11. You overhear a colleague say to a student, "Why are you
          signing up for algebra? You should be taking wood
          working." What might you say to your colleague in
          light of the NCTM's (1986) Position Paper on the
          Mathematics Education of Underrepresented Groups?

p 88ff

M(v) 12. Briefly describe the *storytelling* and *criticism* approaches
          you might use to help children find the number of ways

to "make fifty cents using half dollars, quarters, dimes, and nickels."

p 84
M(v)　13. How would you answer a parent who questions the time your students spend developing LOGO programs instead of memorizing the basic facts?

p 84ff
H(v)　14. Describe one way that you can meet Ingle's (1988) challenge to use computer technologies as something other than drill and practice of minimal mathematics skills or as sources of entertainment.

p CD
H(v)　15. What are some steps a faculty can take to ensure that the best mathematics education possible is accessible to all students, but especially for those with limited English proficiency?

p CD
H(v)　16. How might a school district determine that all schools in the district are taking the effective steps called for in question #15?

p 90
H(s)　17. The following task is written in a field independent mode. Redesign the task so that it is suitable for a student who prefers a field dependent approach.

_____　　+　　_____　=　_____

p 90ff
H(v)　18. What would be the rationale for engaging your students in a project similar to the MAC-mathics Program used in the Chicago Public Schools?

p 70ff
H(v) 19. Why is important for teachers to be knowledgeable of
the history of mathematics that includes the
contributions of many cultures and peoples?

p 75 ff
H(v) 20. How might you use this knowledge (question #19) in
teaching measurement?

== Cover Up Next Portion When Copying Test ==

ANSWERS TO HIGHER LEVEL QUESTIONS

L(s) 1. multiculturalism and equity

M(v) 7. Students' answers may vary but the points made should
clearly indicate an understanding of ready accessibility and
equity issues.

M(v) 8. Students' answers should indicate an understanding of the
problems involved in interpreting syntax of sentence
structure, and "variable-reversal error."

M(v) 9. Students' answers may vary, but consequences similar to
those given in the position paper should be considered.

M(v) 10. Students are not expected to include all underrepresented
groups in the grant proposal, but one or more of the
following groups should be included: females, African
Americans, language minority students, Native
Americans, rural students.

M(v) 11. Answers will vary, but the responses should be in keeping
with the NCTM position paper, including such points as
making a commitment to eliminate psychological, social,
or institutional barriers in the study of mathematics.

M(v) 12. Answers will vary, but students should approximate the
storytelling approach described in the activity on page 88.

M(s) 13. Answers will vary, but students should articulated their
reasons in such a way that it is clear they understand the
purpose of using Logo -- to enhance and strengthen
mathematical reasoning, and mathematical power -- as
well as to give students a sense of accomplishment.

H(v) 14. Answers may vary, but students should clearly indicate their understanding of the uses of technology in information management and exchange.

H(v) 15. Answers may vary, but the points addressed in this chapter, including access, equity, varied strategies, counseling, program evaluation, should be clearly articulated.

H(v) 16. Answers may vary, but students should indicate clearly their understanding of the importance of district-wide program review and evaluation.

H(s) 17. Students' answers should indicate that the revised task would show a separation of the figures into two sets, and the request to "Finish all the number combinations using all of the picture below."

H(v) 18. Answers may vary, but students should include an appreciation of the value of engaging students in writing about mathematics in ways that are true to their real life experiences.

H(v) 19. Answers may vary, but student responses should clearly state their understanding of the importance and necessity of relating mathematics meaningfully in a culturally diverse society.

H(v) 20. Answers may vary, but student responses could develop any of the topics and cultural influences mentioned throughout this chapter -- e.g., cooking and the metric system, area and Tanzanian architecture, etc.

TEST QUESTIONS -- CHAPTER 4

p 102
L()

1. Romberg, Wilson, and Khaketla's study (1989) found a low match of content described in the NCTM Standards and content of the tests in the area(s) of:
    a. problem solving
    b. computation
    c. reasoning
    d. communication

p 102
L(d)

2. A major concern of educators involves the _____ of state-comparative data by federal, state, and local policymakers.
    a. publication
    b. analysis
    c. gathering
    d. misuse

p 103
L()

3. Many of the states' new assessment systems are
    a. aligned with the NCTM Standards
    b. aligned with state systemic initiative programs
    c. limited in state-to-state comparability
    d. mandated

p 104
M(s)

4. There are at least six audiences that expect to receive information from authentic assessments: students, parents, teachers, administrators, the public. Discuss briefly what each audience can expect to be provided by alternative assessments.

p 107
M(v)

5. Discuss briefly the six criteria for judging the quality of mathematics assessment as delineated by the NCTM Assessment Standards.

p 107
M(v)

6. Describe the six characteristics of alternative assessment and the challenge(s) they present to you as a first year teacher.

p 108ff
M()   7. Among the assessment strategies that are being used in
            alternative assessments are:
            a. multiple choice questions
            b. observations
            c. interviews
            d. comprehension questions
            e. self-assessment

p 113ff
M(v)   8. Describe briefly some of the issues facing teachers who
            want to develop performance tasks and open-ended
            tasks that meet the criteria of "authentic assessment."

p 117
L(ho)   9. The following is an example of a(n) _____ scoring
            scale:
            0   Blank paper
                Numbers from problem recopied -- no understanding of
                problem evidenced
                Incorrect answer and no work shown
            1   Inappropriate strategy started -- problem not finished
                Approach unsuccessful -- different approach not tried
                Attempt failed to reach a subgoal
            2   Inappropriate strategy -- but showed some understanding
                of the problem
                Appropriate strategy used -- did not find the solution or
                reached a subgoal but did not finish the problem
                Correct answer and no work shown
            3   Appropriate strategy but
                -- ignored a condition in the problem
                -- incorrect answer for no apparent reason
                -- thinking process unclear
            4   Appropriate strategy or strategies
                Work reflects understanding of problem
                Incorrect answer due to a copying or computational error
            5   Appropriate strategy or strategies
                Work reflects understanding of the problem
                Correct answer

p 117ff
H(v)   10. Describe at least three benefits to using rubrics in scoring
             assessment tasks.

p 119
H(v)   11. Several national educational organizations have issued
             standards for determining teacher competence in

C - 4.2

student assessment. Choose two of the standards and discuss what impact those standards will have on you as you prepare to enter the teaching profession.

p
H(v)   12. Consider the following problem:
The product of two consecutive natural numbers is 1056. Find the sum of these two numbers.

A student solved this problem using the guess-and-check strategy. This student tried several combinations:

10 X 100 = 1000	25 X 26 = 650	31 X 32 = 992
55 X 56 = 3080	30 X 31 = 930	32 X 33 = 1056
	35 X 36 = 1260	

> Then the student wrote   32 X 33   to indicate the answer.

How do you evaluate this answer? Use the scoring scale shown in question #9. Explain why you give the rating you do. What would you say about this student's problem solving abilities?

== Cover Up Next Portion When Copying Test ==

ANSWERS TO HIGHER LEVEL QUESTIONS

L()   1. a, c, d

L()   3. a, b, c, d

M(s)   4. Basically, students should recognize these expectations:
students -- information about themselves as learners
parents -- information about their children's progress, competence, and abilities
teachers -- information to make informed decisions about the next instruction steps
administrators -- information about the effectiveness of the school/district's mathematics program (curriculum)

public -- information about the effectiveness of the school's educational system

M(v)   5. Answers will vary in the discussion of the criteria but should include the six criteria as found in the text on p. 107.

M(v)   6. Answers will vary in the challenge(s) facing them as first year teachers but they should include the characteristics found in the text on p. 107.

M()   7. b, c, e

M(v)   8. Answers will vary but among the issues that can be discussed are diversity, gender, socioeconomic levels, appropriate language, appropriate context, and interest level.

H(v)   10. Answers will vary but may include such ideas as: rubrics are the criteria that describe levels of performance or understanding; they provide students with the expectations of what will be assessed as well as the standards that need to be met; they increase the consistency in the rating of performances, products, and understandings; they provide students with information about where they are in relation to where they need to be.

H(v)   11. Answers will vary but students should choose from among the standards listed in the text on p. 119.

H(v)   12. Answers will vary. Arguments can be made to support a 2 (reached a subgoal but did not find the solution) or 3 (ignored a condition in the problem). The student should be given credit if good reasoning is used in explaining the rating given.

TEST QUESTIONS -- CHAPTER 5

p CD
L(a)

1. A quadrilateral that has at least one pair of opposite sides parallel and the nonparallel sides are congruent
   a. isosceles trapezoid
   b. regular parallelogram
   c. rhombus
   d. any regular polygon

pCD
L(b)

2. The logo procedure, TRI, makes a (an) _____ triangle.
   ```
   TO TRI
   REPEAT 3 [FD 30 RT 120]
   END
   ```
   a. obtuse scalene
   b. acute equilateral
   c. acute isosceles
   d. right isosceles

p133
M(v)

3. Give the directions for connecting points that will create each of the following figures on a geoboard or geoboard paper:
   a. obtuse scalene triangle
   b. acute equilateral triangle
   c. acute isosceles triangle
   d. right isosceles triangle

p133
M(s)

4. Sketch and label each triangle from problem #3 on the dot grid below.

p130
L(a,c)

5. The following two-dimensional pattern when folded makes a solid known as a:

a. tetrahedron
b. triangular pyramid
c. triangular prism
d. truncated tetrahedron

pCD
M(v)   6. Tell everything you can about this figure:

p143
L(d)   7. Which one of the following statements is true:
a. Polygons with the same area will have the same perimeter.
b. Polygons with the same perimeter will have the same area.
c. All perimeters may be found using the formula, $a^2 + b^2 = c^2$.
d. Perimeter and area are not dependent upon each other.

p127
M(b)   8. The Dutch educators, Pierre van Hiele and Dina van Hiele-Geldof, have outlined five levels of development in geometry. When a student can see that a scalene triangle is different from an isosceles and right triangle but knows that a scalene triangle can be defined as a triangle along with the isosceles and right triangle, the student is at the level of _____.
a. rigor
b. abstraction
c. deduction
d. analysis

p127
M()   9. Match the statement with the level of development as defined by the van Hieles.

_____ 1. "Each of these is a different type of triangle, but all these figures are triangles." (Looking at acute, obtuse and right triangles.

_____ 2. "It looks like a stop sign." (Describing an octagon)

_____ 3. "It has 3 sides and 3 angles." (Describing a triangle)

a. Visualization
b. Analysis
c. Abstraction
d. Deduction
e. Rigor

p136
H(s)

10. Use the pictures of attribute pieces below to form a one-or-two-difference train. The train has been started for you. Finish the train and fill in the appropriate word which describes it.

(The attribute pieces are labeled like those in Appendix A.)

LRT LYT LBT LRC LYC LBC LRS LYS LBS

LRR LYR LBR LRH LYH LBH

SRT SYT SBT SRS SYS SBS SRC SYC SBC SRH SYH SBH

SRR SYR SBR

This is a _____ difference train.

| LRT | LYC | ? | LBS | SYS |

p146
H(v)

11. A student uses a protractor to measure the following angles. For Angle A the student records a measure of 80° and 105° for Angle B. Analyze this student's work.

ANGLE A   ANGLE B

p131ff
H(v)   12. Briefly describe the contributions of two different
          cultures to the field of geometry. At what point in the
          study of geometry might you encourage your students to
          learn more about this?

p147
M(b)   13. If student 1 is a field independent learner, which
          method is s/he more likely to use to find the area of the
          triangle?

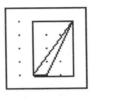

Method A   Method B

p141ff
H(s)   14. Think of the 12 different arrangements of pentominoes
          that you have worked with in Chapter 5. What is the
          pattern that would be able to predict how many
          hexominoes and heptominoes one could make? This is
          where simplifying the problem is an excellent strategy.
          Think of triominoes, quadominoes and pentominoes.
          Their positions are more easily found. Remember
          rotations, flips, and slides do not count as new positions.

	_____ominoes to be made				
	tri	quad	pent	hex	hept
possible arrange- ments			12		
differ. between arrange.	+ _ _ _	+ _ _ _	+ _ _ _	+ _ _ _	
differ. between levels		+ _ _ _	+ _ _ _	+ _ _ _	

p144
H(s)   15. The units marked on the geoboard changes the square
          unit of measure from that which was presented in

C - 5.4

Chapter 5. This one is now equal to one square unit of area. Set up three tables. The tables need to show the relationship of nails that touch (T) and inside nails (I) to area (A) if the inside nails are held constant in one table, and the touching nails are held constant in another table. Every nail that the geoband touches should be counted as a touching nail. Give three examples on each table and predict an area from each table. Use the tables that you construct to find the appropriate formula for each set. (Sample format: A = ___) Use T, I, and A in your formula. The tables have been started for you. After you have found each individual formula, use that information to find one over-all formula that would include all the information gathered in the activity.

A	T	I
	3	0
	4	0
	5	0
Pre dict	8	

A	T	I
	3	1
	4	1
	5	1
Pre dict	9	

A	T	I
	8	0
	8	1
	8	2
Pre dict		6

The formula is _____

The formula is _____

The formula is _____

The general, over-all formula is _____

pCD
M(c)   16. In the Logo program, POLY, the following sets of commands made symmetrical polygons:

POLY 5 1   POLY 8 3
POLY 5 4   POLY 8 5

All of the following sets would be symmetrical except:
a. POLY 4 3 and POLY 4 1
b. POLY 5 2 and POLY 5 3
c. POLY 4 8 and POLY 4 2
d. POLY 5 1 and POLY 5 4

H(v) 17. A second grade class was given the following task on an end of unit assessment in geometry. For each student, describe what the student knows about the figure chosen and what misconceptions are evident. What teaching steps would you take to correct these misconceptions?

> Pick a shape from the board. Write the name of your shape.
>
> Draw it.
>
> Describe it. Write at least three sentences.

Each of the students below chose the triangle as their shape and drew the same basic shape:

Student 1: My shape has three sides. It has three corners. It has zero square quornes. It is spost to has start sides. It's called a shape.

Student 2: This wonderful shape has 3 cutes. It has 3 sides too! All of the sides are not the same lenght

Student 3: It has 3 coners and 3 sides. It's tall and nerow at the top. It's wide at the bodom.

Student 4: It has three corners. It has three sids. It is varey difrentt fram the oters. the triangle is shaped like a cowns hat. And it allso lookes like a ice cream cown. It is a cool shap.

Student 5: I has 3 sides. It looks like a peamode. In some cases it looks like a tenit.

H(v) 18. A fourth grade class had the following task on a unit assessment in geometry. Create a scoring guide, or rubric, for the task and anchor papers for outstanding, adequate, and inadequate responses. (An anchor paper is a exemplar or model response corresponding to the top, middle, and low-end of the scoring guide or rubric criteria.)

You will need the pattern block pieces, a ruler, and a pencil for the following task.

1. Use one trapezoid and three triangles to make a hexagon.

2. Use three rhombus pieces to make a hexagon.

3. Are these hexagons in #1 and #2 congruent? Explain why you think they are or are not congruent.

4. Trace the yellow hexagon in the space below. Use a ruler to draw all the lines symmetry you can find. How many lines of symmetry did you draw?

== Cover Up Next Portion When Copying Test ==

ANSWERS TO HIGHER LEVEL QUESTIONS

M(v) 3. Answers will vary, but the accuracy can be verified by the sketches

M(s) 4. given in response to #4. These sketches are to be based on answers given in question #3.

M(v) 6. As a minimum, students should be able to identify the figure as a closed polygon, an irregular pentagon, with one line of symmetry. Additional information may include such things as: the 2 base angles both seem to be right angles, that of the three remaining angles two seem to be obtuse angles, and one, an acute angle. The sum of the interior angles is 540 degrees. Credit should be given for all correct information.

M( ) 9. 1. b   2. c   3. a

H(s) 10. Answers will vary. For instance, The third car could have any one of three pieces in it: **SBC, LRH** or **LRR**. This is a two difference train. It may also be seen as a one-likeness train. Likenesses are generally more difficult to see for children and were not presented as such in the text.

H(v) 11. College students answers may vary, but the analysis should indicate that the student in question seems to be reading the wrong scales. Possible sequential developmental steps to take would be to 1) visually identify the angles as less than or greater than 90 degrees, 2) use a protractor with only one set of scales to begin with, 3) verify that the student understands the correct placement of the protractor on the angle, etc.

H(v) 12. Students answers may vary, but should indicate a knowledge and appreciation of the contributions made by other cultures in geometry, and an awareness of the appropriate levels at which children might engage in their own research.

H(s) 14. The pattern is shown below. Hexominoes have 23 possible arrangements while heptominoes have 38.

	_____ominoes to be made				
	tri	quad	pent	hex	hept
possible arrange- ments	2	5	12	23	38
differ. between arrange.	+_3__	+_7__	+_11__	+_15__	
differ. between levels	+__4_	+__4_	+__4_		

H(s) 15. The tables show the relationship of nails that touch (T) and inside nails (I) to area (A) when the inside nails are held constant in one table, and the touching nails are held constant in the other table. Three examples must be given on each table, plus the predicted variable. The variables, T, I, and A, must be present in each formula. The over-all formula derived from all the tables is presented below.

A	T	I		A	T	I		A	T	I
1	3	0		3	3	1		6	8	0
2	4	0		4	4	1		8	8	1
3	5	0		5	5	1		10	8	2
Pre dict 6	8	0		Pre dict 9	9	1		Pre dict 18	8	6

C - 5.8

The formula is $A = T - 2 + 1$

The formula is $A = (T)(I)$

The formula is $A = T + 2I - 2$

The general, over-all formula is $A = T + 2(I - 1)$

H(v)   17. Student responses will vary. All of the students have the basic understanding of the triangle having 3 sides and 3 corners. There are some misconceptions related to position, size of angles ("zero square quornes"), and shape ("tall and nerow at the top ... wide at the bodom"). Teaching steps could include using geoboards to "follow the leader" in making shapes, looking for different examples of triangular shapes in the classroom or outside, and similar hands-on and real-life activities.

H(v)   18. Student responses will vary. The rubric or scoring guide should include the elements of the task as described. A critical part of the task, and thus of the rubric, is the communication of reasoning called for in step 3.

TEST QUESTIONS -- CHAPTER 6

p161
L(a)

1. A frequently used name for mass is
   a. weight
   b. capacity
   c. area
   d. volume

p153
L(c)

2. The first known standards of measurement were established in:
   a. 1 A.D.
   b. 3000 B.C.
   c. 6000 B. C.
   d. 10,000 B. C.

p168
L(b)

3. According to the data from the fourth NAEP mathematics assessment (Kouba et al., 1988) _____ correctly identified examples like the one below which asked which of the two containers had the greater capacity for holding water.

   a. 10 percent of third graders
   b. 90 percent of third graders
   c. virtually all first graders
   d. 10 percent of middle school students (grade 7)

p170
L(a/c)

4. Using a calculator, what is the volume of the cone below if the radius is doubled and the height is halved?

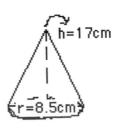

h=17cm

r=8.5cm

a. 2571.14 cubic cm
b. 2571.1367 sq. cm.
c. 2572.44 cu. cm.
d. 1285.5683 cm.

p155
M(v)   5. Native Americans were accomplished mathematicians. Give an example from their known accomplishments that illustrates this.

p164ff
H(s)   6. Using centimeter graph paper, sketch all the possibilities of constructing rectangles with perimeters of 12 cm.

p164ff
M(v)   7. Name a place or object in a typical school that children could best measure in
       a. dekameters   _____

       b. decigrams   _____

       c. milliliters   _____

p173
L(b)   8. The text advocates that children learn to tell time by
       a. starting with a digital clock rather an analog clock.
       b. giving only the minutes after the hour.
       c. introducing a minute face clock first, progressing to an hour and minute face clock second.
       d. teach only the analog clock with no reference to the digital models.

p164
M(c)   9. If a nickel has a weight of 10 grams, how much money would you have if you had a kilogram of nickels?
       a. $50
       b. $500
       c. $5
       d. $5000

CD
M(c)   11. If the answer to the measurement of the figure below is 36 cm., then we are talking about the object's _____.

a. area
b. volume
c. perimeter
d. mass

p166
M(d)   11. Using the following information, find the radius using
        a calculator to help with the calculations:

        Area   Radius
        256.78 cm^2 ?

        The radius is:
        a. 28.395232 cm
        b. 9.0430675 cm^3
        c. 81.77707 cm^2
        d. 9.04 cm

M(a)   12. Use the following Cuisenaire rod models for money:

        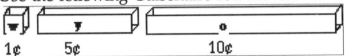

        1¢   5¢   10¢

        Then, this Cuisenaire rod arrangement represents
        _____ in amounts of money.

        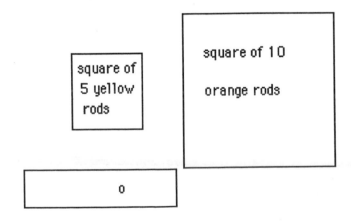

        a. $1.35
        b. $1.15
        c. $.25 + $.50 + $.10
        d. $.21

p162
M(b)   13. One kilogram is approximately the weight of:
       a. a standard-sized beach ball
       b. a standard-sized Bible
       c. a standard-sized (pullman) suitcase
       d. a new-born infant

p173
M(a)   14. Finish this analogy:
           0 degrees C is to 32 degrees F as 34.8 degrees C is to
           _____ degrees F.
       a. 98.6
       b. 100
       c. 212
       d. 96.8

p174
H(v)   15. In one classroom the teacher distributes a test paper
           that includes a clock face with the directions "Show 7
           o'clock by drawing the hands of the clock." In another
           classroom, the teacher distributes a test paper that
           includes the directions to "Draw a clock face and show
           7 o'clock on it." What might the second teacher learn
           about students' understanding of time that the first
           teacher probably will not learn about his/her students'
           understanding?

p162
H(s)   16. Money is often taught during a unit in measurement.
           If you are teaching coin equivalencies, in what ways
           will this differ from teaching metric equivalencies?

p170ff
H(v)   17. Create three kinds of clocks recommended in Chapter 6
           for the teaching of time in a sequence to children.
           Sketch each one under the designated label. Show what
           the clocks would look like with step 1 being the first
           concept to be taught in the sequence.

           Step 1   Step 2   Step 3

18. Do a field dependent and a field independent measurement of the area for the polygon pictured on the geoboards. Put lines to show how you partitioned the segments in each method. Write the exact measurement with ☐ as one square unit of area under each figure.

Field Dependent

Field Independent

The area is _____

The area is _____

19. Here are several student responses to an assessment item. You have been asked to select an exemplar of a "1" or "Inadequate response" rating; a "3" or "Adequate response" rating; and a "5" or "Excellent response" rating. Indicate your choice of a "1," "3," and "5" exemplar and defend your choice.

> Estimate the number of tiles (1" x 1") of this size that would cover this (8.5" x 11") page.
> Explain your answer.

Student 1: 88 because the sides are about one inch and I know the page is 11 by 8. I mutaplid those numbers to get a answre.

Student 2: 11 x 9 = 99 tiles would cover this paper. I found this answer by measuring the square (tile) and measuring the paper. The tile was 1 inch on each side and the paper was 8.5 in. (short side) and 11 in. (long side). I rounded 8.5 to 9 and then multiplied 11 times nine to come up with the estamation of 99. Then, I checked and double checked my procedure by drawing a line on each side's first inch mark. the result was a tic-tac-toe pattern of squares about the same size as the example. So, I came up with the answer of 99.

Student 3: 101 because the tile is the same size as my two fingers and so I just put my two fingers all along my paper.

Student 4: I estimate that 80 tiles. I just gessed.

Student 5: I say 37 tiles would cover it. I used my two fingers and measured it. Then I moved the measurement around the page.

Student 6: First I lined them down the page and across the page and it was 11 down and 8 across and 11 x 8 = 88 and rounded it to the nearest 10 because were estimating and the answer is 90

Student 7: 80   There is 8 across the top and ten going down.

Student 8: 81   (No written explanation. Rather this student used a ruler and made a grid [9x9] starting below the task description [about 2 inches from the top of the page] and began numbering across the grid .... row 1 was numbered from 1-9, row 2 from 10-18, row 3 from 19-27, and row 4 from 28 to 32. None of the other boxes were numbered.

== Cover Up Next Portion When Copying Test ==

ANSWERS TO HIGHER LEVEL QUESTIONS

M(v) 5. Answers will vary. Examples that students might cite include, systems of measures accurate enough to permit the building of highways across mountains and rough terrain, precise calendars, geometrical developments, etc.

H(s) 6. Using centimeter graph paper, the following shows all the possibilities of constructing rectangles with perimeters of 12 cm.

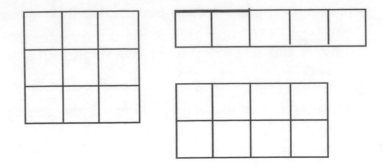

M(v) 7. Answers will vary. Typical answers might include:
dekameters: hallway, width of gym floor
decigrams: pencils, board erasers, notebooks
milliliters: glass of water, can of pop

H(v) 15. Answers will vary. Points that students should be aware
of: importance of even spacing of numerals, placement of
hands in the center, etc.

H(s) 16. Students answers will vary, but a primary difference that
all should be aware of is the lack of physical relationship
among coins. Ten mm can be shown to be physically
equivalent to 1 cm on a ruler or meterstick, but ten
pennies do not have the physical value of one dime.
Thus, a teacher can ask, "How many millimeters are in a
centimeter?," but should ask "How many pennies does it
take to equal the value of a dime?" rather than "How
many pennies are in a dime?"

H(v) 17. The exact drawing of each clock will vary, but the criteria
found under each step should be seen in each drawing
made by the student.

Step 1	Step 2	Step 3
Begin with only an hour face clock; no other hands should be on it. Only the numbers 1 to 12 should appear.	Introduce the minute hand, showing only the hour and half hour times.	The clock should have added five-minute intervals. Children should only be asked to give minutes after the hour.

H(s) 18. A field-dependent and a field-independent measurement
of the area for the polygon is shown below. The lines are
partitioned in the segments that must be shown for each

method. The exact measurement must be stated using the word, <u>square</u> units to show that the college student understands the correct way to measure area.

Field Dependent Method

Field Independent Method

$1 + 1 + 1 + .5 = 3.5$
The area is <u>3.5 sq. units</u>.

$9 - (2 + 2.5 + 1) = 3.5$
The area is <u>3.5 sq. units</u>.

H(v) 19. Answers will vary. Consider the college student's reasons for the ratings. For instance, Student 5 is the most likely exemplar of a "1" rating. Although there was a strategy, it was not effective for the task and the result is not "in the ballpark." Student 3 used a similar strategy but is more within the ballpark.

Student 2 is the most verbal and many may choose this for the "5" exemplar. The "check and double check" of the procedure is a more detailed explanation than any of the other responses. Student 1 may also be a candidate for the "5" exemplar.

Student 8 demonstrated a strategy that was not fully carried out but the result is within the ballpark.

P 192
L(b) 1. Which order does the development of counting follow?

a	b
The order differs for	rote counting
each child.	rational counting
	counting with meaning

c	d
rational counting	counting with meaning
rote counting	rote counting
counting with meaning	rational counting

P192
L(c) 2. Counting becomes meaningful around the age of _:
   a. two
   b. four
   c. six
   d. eight

P188
L(d) 3. The symbols, + and -- , should be introduced to children:
   a. before class inclusion activities but after classification tasks
   b. after number conservation is established but before sorting begins
   c. before sorting objects by more or less and before calculator activities start
   d. after number conservation and equivalence of number is established.

P191ff
M( ) 4. Match the brief description or examples in the left column with the name of the counting strategy each represents from the right column by writing the letter of the appropriate strategy to the left of each example.

1. Children who exhibit this strategy say the numbers in the proper sequence (up to ten or so) but can't always coordinate the saying of the number names with the objects being counted.

a. Skip counting

b. Counting back

2. Here, correct number names are given as the child counts from any starting point, counting: "... nine, ten, eleven, ..." or "... eighty-nine, ninety, ninety-one,..."; an essential strategy in developing addition skills

c. Point counting

d. Rote counting

3. The child counts by twos, fives, etc. from any point in either direction; provides valuable readiness for multiplication and division.

e. Counting on

4. Probably the first stage in which all four basic principles of counting are exhibited by the child.

f. Rational counting

P191
M(b) 5. Which of these would be an appropriate pattern sequence to show to children?
    a. Ø   Ø
    b. ®   ®   ®
    c. R B R B R B R B
    d. snap, clap, snap, clap

P182

M(a,d) 6. According to Hiebert and Lindquist (1990), a teacher who wants to help children build conceptual knowledge would do which of the following in introducing addition:
a. talk about children joining other children at the swing set
b. have children fill in an addition chart for seatwork
c. have flashcards of addition facts in a learning center
d. provide animal counters for acting out "zoo" problems

P188

M(c) 7. A teacher sets out a row of 7 unifix cubes. Below it she starts a second row but places only 2 unifix cubes in the row. A student who can complete the second row, so that it also has 7 cubes, is demonstrating an understanding of:
a. seriation
b. classification
c. equivalence of sets
d. number conservation

P184ff

M() 8. A student who can say, "All the black beads are plastic but not all the plastic beads are black," understands the concept of _____ and is ready to learn to count ___ _____.

a. seriation
b. reversibility

c. class inclusion

d. back from 11-1
e. the entire set, beginning at one and going to eleven
f. from 7, "8...9...10...11"

P191

M(b) 9. A child is counting a collection of shells and begins by touching each shall as the number is said. After eight, the child continues to count but faster so the counting is not in a matched relationship with the shells. Which concept or concepts does the child understand?
a. rational counting
b. rote counting
c. counting with meaning
d. a and b

P187

M(c) 10. The child says that the chips in Figure A do not have the same number as the chips in Figure B. The child is having difficulty understanding:

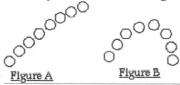

Figure A   Figure B

    a. rote counting of number
    b. equivalence of number
    c. conservation of number
    d. b and c

P183

M(b) 11. Look at the following sets. Which sets would most likely be sorted by the average preschooler or kindergartner as discussed in Chapter 7?

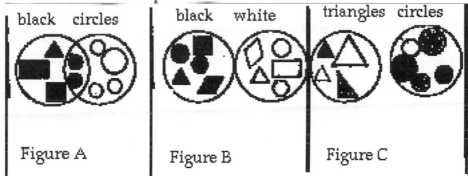

    a. Figure A
    b. Figure B
    c. Figure A and Figure B
    d. Figure B and Figure C

P186

M(a) 12. Seriation is to cardinal and ordinal number as sorting objects is to ____.
    a. graphing
    b. equivalency of number
    c. class inclusion
    d. b and c

P181

L(a,d) 13. The two dimensions that define developmentally appropriate activities, according to the NAEYC (1988) are _____ and _____.

a. age
b. physical
c. social
d. individual

P183

M(c) 14. The following attribute pieces were shown to a student with the directions to place all the blue squares in a set together.

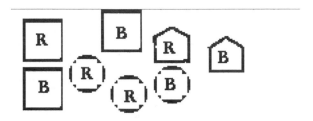

The student chose the following pieces:

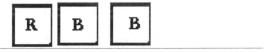

The student does not understand:
a. number conservation when eight things are shown
b. class inclusion of three or more attributes
c. classification by a consistent sorting criterion
d. a and b

P195

M(a) 15. A child in your classroom writes the number, fourteen, as 41 and the number 9 as P. As the teacher you need to prepare materials that allow the child to practice:
a. tactile experiences with verbal structures in number sequences
b. place value understanding
c. number conservation tasks
d. class inclusion and flexible number patterns

P

H(v) 16. Design a lesson for one of the early number concepts from this chapter that incorporates a multicultural aspect.

P184

H(v) 17. Design an activity that will allow children to sort objects in more than one way. Show you know the four standards for sorting materials by including all four in your directions for the activity as you would use them with children.

P188
& CD
H(v) 18. Using a calculator with a constant feature, design a lesson to teach "one more" and "one less" with materials that will be of interest to kindergarten and early primary children.

P187
H(v) 19. Create an activity sequence that will teach seriation with Cuisenaire rods as the teaching material, using the model of James Heddens (Chapter 2) to structure the activity. Indicate how the activity corresponds with each part of the Heddens model.

H(v) 20. A part of a lesson plan created by methods student for a kindergarten class is shown here. Identify the tasks, the opportunities for discourse, and elements of the learning environment. Do they measure up to the Standards?

Objective: The students will recognize and identify numerals with 90% accuracy.

Teaching/Learning Activities: 1. I will read a book called "A-Counting We Will Go," to the class and then as a class we will count the objects pictured in the book.

2. As a class, the children will be given "number cards," which are usually used for attendance, and they will be given some "think time" to count the objects on their card.

3. Then I will say the number 1 through 19 and when his/her number is called, each child will give me his/her "number card."

4. I will ask each student to match the number of objects, he/she has on a notecard, with the numerals placed in front of them.

5. Once a student matches his/her card correctly to the numeral, he/she will clap that many times.

6. Once each student has matched his/her card with the numerals, each child will take the card that they had back to his/her seat. There they will write down the numeral that matches the number of objects on his/her card.

7. After each child has finished writing his/her number on the other card, I will come around and put a sticker on the cards that have the correct numeral on them. If there is an incorrect number, I will ask the child to count the objects again and once they get the right number, I will put a sticker on his/her card.

===== Cover Up Next Portion When Copying Test =====

ANSWERS TO HIGHER LEVEL QUESTIONS

M( ) 4.   <u>d</u> 1.   <u>e</u> 2.   <u>a</u> 3.   <u>f</u> 4.

M() 8.   b, c, f

H(v) 16. Answers will vary ... The college student should be able to design a lesson that draws upon multicultural aspects such as literature, art, and/or history.

H(v) 17. The activity design will vary . . . Answers must include the four standards required in a sorting activity:
a. using an area with a defined boundary
b. using different sorting criteria
c. asking what rule is being followed
d. using flexible examples

H(v) 18. Answers will vary . . . The college student must design a lesson which clearly demonstrates the specific keys to press on a calculator to obtain the desired results as a kindergarten or early primary child would do the activity.

H(v) 19. Answers will vary . . . The seriation activity with Cuisenaire rods must show the progression from Step 1 through step 4 of the Heddens model. Each step must be labeled correctly with directions showing how the steps fit the Heddens model. The steps are:
Step 1: Concrete (actual Cuisenaire rods)
Step 2: Semi-concrete (picture of Cuisenaire rods)
Step 3: Semi-abstract (stylized rods; different length tally marks for rods)
Step 4: Abstract (only numerals or letters to stand for each rod)

H(v) 20. Answers will vary somewhat. Among the tasks described in this lesson plan are: counting the objects pictured in the book, counting the objects on a number card, recognizing the number on the card when the number word is spoken, matching objects to a number on a card, clapping the number of times on the card, and writing the numeral that matches the number of objects on the card.

As the lesson plan is written there does not seem to be any consideration given to discourse.

In terms of the environment, there is no indication that students will be doing any type of paired or collaborative work. There is an attempt to use physical objects, body movement (clapping), visual and auditory senses.

Some students may also recognize that the objective is not aligned with the activities ... recognizing and identifying numerals 1-10 ... the numbers go through 19, students must be able to write a numeral.

On the whole this lesson is weak in terms of the Standards in the limited worthwhile-ness of the tasks, the lack of discourse, and the limited learning environment.

TEST QUESTIONS -- CHAPTER 8

P205
L(a,c)   1. The NCTM curriculum standards (1989) stress the need for
             students to develop an understanding of:
             a. the underlying structures of arithmetic of fractions, decimals,
                 and integers
             b. addition and subtraction in different bases over ten
             c. the nature of place value as the first property of the number
                 system

P221
L(a)   2. If a child writes eighteen as 81, the child is probably confusing:
            a. place value with name value
            b. conservation of number with seriation
            c. place value
            d. name value

P207
& CD
M(b)   3. Which base does this partial numeral strip represent

	4	3
	4	4
	4	5
	5	0
	5	1
	5	2
	5	3
	5	4
	5	5
1	0	0
1	0	1
1	0	2
1	0	3
1	0	4

            a. base $_{five}$
            b. base$_{six}$
            c. base$_{seven}$
            d. base$_{ten}$

P207
&CD
M(s)
4. Continue this numeral strip for the base you identified above in #4.

$$5 \quad 4 \quad 5$$

–	–	–	–
–	–	–	–
–	–	–	–
–	–	–	–
–	–	–	–
–	–	–	–
–	–	–	–
–	–	–	–

P207
&CD
M(s)
5. Using multi-base blocks, draw the representation for 2101_{five}.

P207
&CD
M(b)
6. The base seven representation of the numeral in #7 would be:
   a. 2103_{seven}
   b. 1561_{seven}
   c. 256_{seven}
   d. 514_{seven}

P211
M(c)
7. The purpose of "Wipeout," a game for calculators, is to subtract the required place value amount to reduce that place to zero. For instance, if you enter "34" in your calculator, to wipeout the "3" you must subtract 30. Now, enter the number one million, four hundred fifty-six thousand, thirty-two in the calculator. If you wipeout the "one" and the "six," what numeral will then be displayed on your calculator.
   a. forty-five thousand, thirty-two
   b. four thousand, five hundred thirty-two
   c. four hundred fifty thousand, thirty-two
   d. four hundred fifty thousand, two

P220
M(a)
8. This number, 271, 000,000,000,000,000,000,000,000 is read as:
   a. two hundred seventy-one septillion

b. two hundred seventy-one zillion
c. two hundred and seventy-one septillion
d. two hundred and seventy-one octillion

P223
M(s)   9. Using base 10 blocks, draw an illustration of 1.035.

P220
M(v)   10. Suppose the following article appeared in the local paper:

IP: Anywhere, The Globe
Queen Bernada of the Northlands told 700 delegates and observers at a 10-day session of the Convention on International Trade in Endangered Species that action must be taken now to save wildlife and the environment.
Delegates from 103 convention nations must decide whether to leave endangered species under their present designation with a limit of 2 animals per license or to ban all hunting of endangered species.
Ewbabzim says it earns $9 million a year by selling tusks from herds, estimated at 52,000. Tusks fetch more than $300 a kilogram on the world market. Hides can bring up to $50 a square meter.
Environmentalists say poachers kill at least 70,000 endangered species and that herds have been reduced continent-wide from 1.3 million in a decade to just more than 600,000 and can only be protected by a ban that prohibits the sale of all tusks and hides.

List a) three numbers which are reported exactly: _____
_____
b) 2 numbers which may have been rounded to simplify the information: _____
c) 3 different estimates: _____

P211
M(s)   11. On the next page are pictures of proportional and non-proportional models of the place value system. Rank from greatest to least the models that show the greatest proportionality to those that show the least or no proportionality.

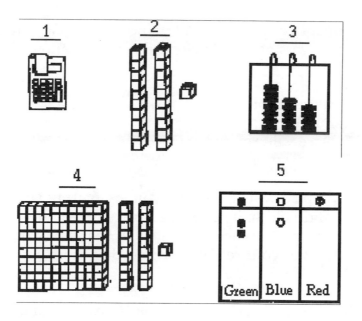

P204ff

M(v)   12. How would you explain to your 6th grade class that $(50)^0 = 1$?

CD

M(s)   13. Use your calculator to figure out the base ten numeral for the early Babylonian number, given the chart at the left.

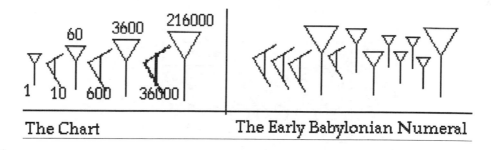

The Chart   The Early Babylonian Numeral

P204ff

M(b)   14. Do the following activity as a mental math exercise. Analyze what properties and operations you needed to know in order to do the activity.

 You have chosen three number tiles. One tile has a seven on it; another tile has a two, and third tile has a five. Make a number that is greater than three hundred but less than seven hundred. Take the largest number of the two possibilities and increase the number by 200. Decrease the number by 100.

The number is _____, and you could not have done this problem unless you understood the classification of the _____ ____.

   a. 627; numeration system
   b. 672; number system
   c. 527; place value systems
   d. 672; numeration system

P225
H(v)   15. For work on place value concepts you are pairing your field-dependent and field-independent learners. Describe two different activities (one appropriate for each style) that you would provide for each pair, and your reasons for selecting those activities.

P211ff
H(s)   16. Design a bean stick manipulative based on the examples seen in Chapter 8. Show the bean sticks needed to represent the numeral 2C in base fifteen.

P211ff
H(s)   17. Regroup the set of chips in base fourteen on the chip trading till and write the answer in numerals, indicating the correct base as a part of the subscript of the numeral. Show any exchanges needed by ringing the set to be exchanged and using an arrow to show the resulting action. Let the letters of the alphabet in their normal order represent any additional numerals you may need.

The numeral is _____ .

CD
H(s)   18. Analyze the multi-base blocks shown on the number line below. Write in the corresponding numeral below each point. The first numeral has been done for you. Create the last set of multi-base

blocks and write its numeral underneath the line. This whole number one of blocks is in base _____

100

Key:
Flat = ☐   Block = ⬜   Long Block = ⬛
Draw the rest of the blocks in size proportion to these.

H(v)   19. A fifth grade teacher is teaching a lesson on place value. Students are rolling six number cubes and creating numbers. The first student to roll the number cubes makes the largest possible number. The second student to roll makes the smallest possible number. Every student who rolls now tries to make a number in between the largest and smallest numbers. What are 3 questions to encourage student-student discourse that this teacher could pose to the class?

===== Cover Up Next Portion When Copying Test =====

ANSWERS TO HIGHER LEVEL QUESTIONS

M(s)   3.

$$
\begin{array}{ccc}
 & 5\ 4\ 5 \\
- & \underline{5\ 5\ 0} \\
- & \underline{5\ 5\ 1} \\
- & \underline{5\ 5\ 2} \\
- & \underline{5\ 5\ 3} \\
- & \underline{5\ 5\ 4} \\
 & \underline{5\ 5\ 5} \\
1\ & \underline{0\ 0\ 0} \\
1\ & \underline{0\ 0\ 1} \\
1\ & 0\ 0\ 2 \\
\end{array}
$$

M(s)   5. The multi-base blocks drawn should consist of 2 BLOCKS, 1 FLAT, no LONGS, and 1 UNIT.

M(v)   9. The base 10 block illustration of 1.0351 could consist of 1 BLOCK, no FLATS, 3 LONGS, and 5 small BLOCKS (units) or 1 FLAT, no LONGS, 3 small BLOCKS (units) and 5 "small" FLATS (as seen on text page 223). Any block can be used as the unit block, and the remaining blocks must simply be of the correct amount and right proportion.

M(v) 10. The following numbers can be identified as: <u>exact:</u> 10, 103, 12; <u>rounded:</u> 700, 9 million, 1.3 million, 600,000, 70,000 <u>estimates:</u> 52,000, $300, $50

M(v) 12. Answers will vary. Students may illustrate the concept with reference to models of the numeration system, or informal proof. Their explanations should be mathematically correct and in keeping with middle school students' reasoning and understanding.

H(v) 15. Answers may vary. The activities that the students describe and their reasoning for choosing them should be in keeping with, but not limited to, those described on text page 225.

H(s) 16. The beanstick manipulative should look like the one pictured below for the numeral 2C in base fifteen.

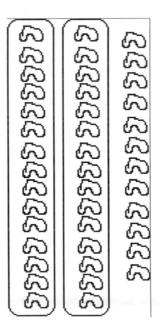

H(s) 17. The chip trading till should look like the one below. Note that the student may add any color to the next column as long as it is not a color which has been used before.

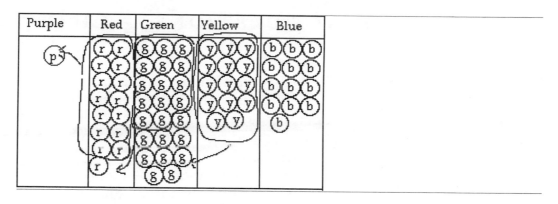

The numeral is 12A0D$_{fourteen}$

H(s)   18. The number line is in base two. The student should have drawn
a FLAT BLOCK as the last set of blocks to fit the pattern in base
two. The number line shows the manipulatives needed to count
by FLATS in base two. It is the equivalent of counting by
hundreds in the base ten system. The answer in numerals appear
below each set of blocks.

H(v)   19. Answers will vary.

P232
L(a,b) 1. The NCTM curriculum standards (1989) advocates that teachers should provide experiences to develop "operation sense." This term means:
   a. understanding properties and relationships for each operation
   b. developing relationships among operations
   c. The curriculum standards did not address this issue.

P235
L(c)   2. The ____ concept of subtraction closely related to 1-1 relationships is_____.
   a. missing addend
   b. completion
   c. comparison
   d. take away.

P238
L(c)   3. When the number of objects in the original set and the number of new sets to be formed are known, this is called:
   a. associative multiplication
   b. measurement division
   c. partitive division
   d. Cartesian product multiplication

P256
L(c)   4. In Chapter 9, speed tests over the basic facts are advocated if:
   a. teachers allow 2 minutes at the beginning and reduce time to 1 minute after all facts are learned
   b. tests are given over all the facts as a group from the beginning of instruction
   c. easy facts are learned first, building gradually to the 100 facts
   d. parents work at home using drill cards for all the basic facts over a few weeks

L(s)   5. Three different interpretations for multiplication are

   a._____

   b. _____

   c. _____

P231

L(a)   6. The NCTM curriculum and evaluation standards (1989)
        suggest that children encounter in various problem
        situations the four basic operations beginning at what
        grade level?
        a. kindergarten
        b. first grade for +, - ; 3rd grade for x, --
        c. depends on the operation
        d. depends on the textbook used

P239

M(c)   7. The Cuisenaire rod problem below is read as:

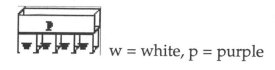 w = white, p = purple

        a. Four sets of white rods equal the purple rod
        b. How many sets of four are there in the purple rod?
        c. Four divided into four sets is one in each set.
        d. a and b

M(d)   8. What is the basic fact combination represented by the
        touch finger math explained in Chapter 7 and shown
        below?

        a. 5 + 3
        b. 6 x 9
        c. 5 x 3
        d. 9 x 9

P246

M(b)   9. The table below teaches the same strategy as:

+	0	1	2	3	4	5	6	7	8	9
0										
1										
2										11
3									11	12
4								11	12	13
5									13	14
6										15
7					11					16
8				11	12	13				17
9			11	12	13	14	15	16	17	

a. the Cuisenaire rod staircase where one white is added on each time
b. the Wirtz 10 trays
c. repeated subtraction with connecting cubes
d. the distributive property with the pan balance

P260

M(b,c)   10. The child who answers

$$\begin{array}{r} 8 \\ -\ 1 \\ \hline 6 \end{array}$$

should be encouraged to use which of the following approaches to help remediate the problem:
a. the counting back strategy
b. the number line if counting only the spaces
c. the derived fact strategies

P251ff

M(c)   11. Which of the students below will learn the basic facts more quickly as suggested by the NCTM curriculum standards (1989) concerning the study of basic fact strategies?

Original Problem: 8 x 9 = ?

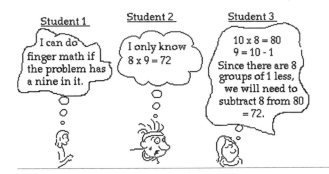

a. Student 1
b. Student 2
c. Student 3
d. All 3 students will learn them equally as quick

P256ff

M(v)   12. A parent of one of your students comes to see you as school. She informs you she wants to help her daughter "learn her facts" so that her daughter will do well in math. What suggestions would you offer this parent?

P250
&CD

H(v)   13. Describe how you might incorporate information about
            mathematics from other cultures in a lesson related to
            exploring the operation of multiplication.

P247ff

II(v)   14. A first grade teacher is introducing the concept of
            subtraction. She puts the following illustration on the
            flannel board and says: "seven take away three is - - -"

        What suggestions would you
        make to this teacher to help her
        develop a lesson more in keeping
        with the NCTM standards (1989)?

P248ff

H(v)   15. Create a multiplication triomino and show the
            resulting basic fact combinations that can be derived
            from it.

P250ff

H(v)   16. Create two models with dominoes being used to teach
            multiplication. In the first model, let each domino
            equal one set. In the second model, let each half of a
            single domino equal one set. In the second model,
            which set of single dominoes will always be used with
            multiplication?

CD

H(s)   17. Use your knowledge of the Logo program, ADD, to
            create new possibilities for extending the numbers that
            can be created for use in new double digit programs:

            In the Logo program, ADD, this pattern is seen . . .
              "1 + RANDOM 10 . . . creates random numbers from 1
              to 10

"2 + RANDOM 10 . . . creates random numbers from 2 to 11
"3 + RANDOM 10 . . . creates random numbers from 3 to 12

Create a minuend and subtrahend of double-digit numbers (using the RANDOM procedure in Logo) where the largest minuend could be 75, the largest subtrahend could be 60, and least difference between them could be 5 and the greatest difference between them could be 30.

Minuend = _____

Subtrahend = _____

H(v) 18. An elementary education preservice teacher is preparing a lesson domino addition for second graders. She plans on modeling two ways of writing number sentences:
a) ___ + ___ = ___   b) ___ and ___ = ___
How might this lead to student-teacher discourse? What other ways would you suggest that she use dominoes for introducing addition?

== Cover Up Next Portion When Copying Test ==

ANSWERS TO HIGHER LEVEL QUESTIONS

L(s) 5. a. repeated addition or grouping
b. combinations, cross multiplication, or Cartesian products
c. arrays

M(v) 12. Answers will vary. The students response should be in keeping with the focus of the NCTM standards, awareness of the necessity of considering individual children's readiness, indicate knowledge of activities that develop and enhance number and operation sense, as well as appropriate memorization activities.

H(v) 13. Answers will vary. Student responses may include information similar to that found on text page 250 or on the CD, but are not limited to that.

H(v)   14. Answers will vary.   Student answers may include ideas
            similar to those found on text pages 247-250. The
            student answers should evidence some awareness of the
            need for tact in addition to knowledge of the Standards
            and appropriate teaching strategies.

H(v)   15. The triominoes will vary but each one should generate
            4 basic number facts, two multiplication facts and two
            division facts as show in the example below:

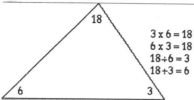

3 x 6 = 18
6 x 3 = 18
18÷6 = 3
18÷3 = 6

H(v)   16. The domino models will vary, but the student should
            realize that since multiplication means how many sets
            of _____ are in the total amount, each domino in
            the first model must have the same number of dots
            although the arrangement of the dots can be different.
            In the second model, only the doubles will be able to be
            used as in the examples below:

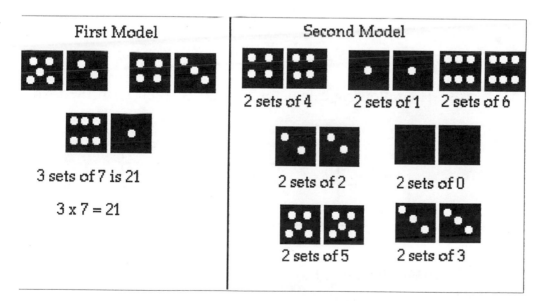

H(s)   17. The answer should be exactly like the answer below:

        Minuend = ___"65 + RANDOM 11
        Subtrahend = _"45 + RANDOM 16

H(v)   18. Answers will vary.

P282
L(a)   1. The copy method of multiplication and division is more
            likely to benefit the _____ learner.
            a. field dependent
            b. field independent
            c. auditory

P290
M(s)   2. Look at the table below:

	== A ==	== B ==	== C ==	== D ==
1	x	?	?	2200
2	38	836	8360	83600
3	380	8360	83600	?
4	3800	83600	836000	?

Without using a calculator, rather by using mental
math, determine the numbers that belong in B1, C1, D3,
and D4. The technique you most probably used is
known as ____.

B1 = _____   D3 = _____

C1 = _____   D4 = _____

Technique: _____

P286
M(d)   3. The following calculator activity is taken from the text:

START

19683	6	9	27
5	4	3	3
18	3	5	6
6	5	3	0.9

END | 9 |

Trace the path to END and describe the reasoning you
used to find that path.

CD
M(b)   4. In the spreadsheet program on the next page, if the
            numbers in row 1 were changed to 60   600   6000
            what would happen to the spreadsheet?

	== A ==	== B ==	== C ==	== D ==
1	Number	10	100	1000
2	243	2430	24300	243000
3	2430	24300	243000	2430000
4	24300	243000	2430000	24300000

   a. All the numbers in the A column would automatically change.

   b. All the numbers in b2 to b4 and c2 to c4 and d2 to d4 would change as the 60, 600, and 6000 are typed into the program.

   c. A new number would be calculated for EACH cell in the spreadsheet.

   d. b and c

P274

M(s)   5. Analyze the manipulatives below. Arrange them in order from most concrete to least concrete.

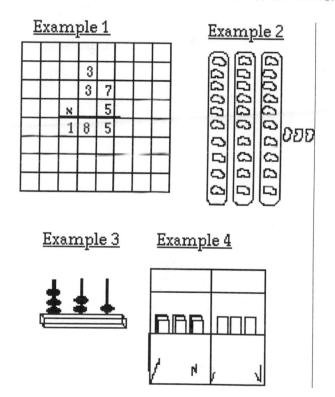

P293ff

M(v)   6. The "Tax Game" in chip trading consists of playing 3 rounds, collecting the number of chips determined by each roll of a die, and making required trades and then on the fourth round, giving back to the bank the number of chips determined by that roll of the die.

Below are the mats of a group of children after 4 rounds. What base (or country) are the children playing in?
_____ What are three questions you might ask of Student A to assess his/her understanding of regrouping in addition/subtraction?

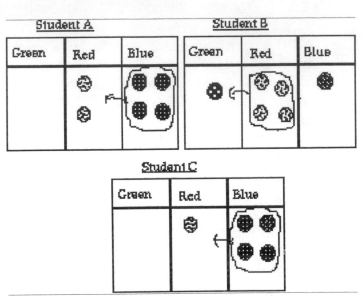

P293ff

M(b)   7. Analyze the work of the student below. Which of the following learning aids would be the best to help the student?

$$
\begin{array}{r}
25 \\
\times\,98 \\
\hline
200 \\
+\,225 \\
\hline
425
\end{array}
$$

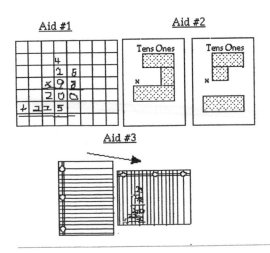

a. Aid #1
b. Aid #2
c. Aid #3
d. a and c

P283
M(12)   8. Use the calculator to figure this problem:
What whole number placed in the blank brings the
estimate closest to the target answer?

$$471 \times \underline{\hspace{1cm}} = 5444$$

P
M(b)   9. Which problem(s) would the NCTM curriculum
standards (1989) recommend as least appropriate for
students to do as a worksheet with pencil and paper?

Example 1   Example 2   Example 3

$$3 \overline{)\, 785}$$ $$39 \overline{)\, 12478}$$ $$40 \overline{)\, 8400}$$

a. Example 1
b. Example 2
c. Example 3

P278
M(v)   10. Describe the teaching procedure to be followed when
teaching comparison subtraction with regrouping.
Write a situational problem, name the materials, and
illustrate the steps you would follow.

CD
M(b)   11. The "Russian Peasant" method of multiplication is
shown below. After analyzing Example A, examine
Example B, and select the next step and the final answer.
Show your work on Example B.

Example A		Example B	
36 x	49	58 x	21
36	49	58	21
18	98	29	42
9	196	14	84
4	392	7	168
2	784	.....	336
1	1568	1	672
	1764		....

```
a. 4,    1218
b. 3,    1218
c. 4,    1398
d. 3,    1398
```

P272ff

H(v)   12. Why might you demonstrate the method shown in #11
            above for your students? What kind of algorithmic
            model is this and why do you classify it as such?

P293ff

H(s/v) 13. A student answers multi-digit addition like the ones
            below. Work the last problem as this student would do
            it. Analyze the error pattern and describe the materials
            and approach you would use to help remediate the
            problem.

```
  i) 532    ii) 65   iii) 157   iv) 653   v) 816
   + 156      + 71      + 894     + 451     + 287
     688        19       9115       114
```

P298

H(s)   14. Analyze the algorithm done by the bright fourth grader.
            It is the same as the one presented in the text. Then do
            the second problem, using the same algorithm as the
            student. Do your work on the answer sheet.

```
        34   R 5                    _____
  23 | 787                    27 | 9 8 2 7
       60
       18
        9
       97
       80
       17
       12
        5
```

H(s)   15. Do each of the two problems below in the copy method
            as described in the text in Chapter 10.

                     23   ‾‾‾‾‾‾
                   x 42   42 | 8 9 5

CD

H(s)   16. Look at the following algorithm for division from an
            1877 textbook. Analyze how the problem is done. Then
            do the problem seen on the right in the same manner.

        From 1877

        Divide 1592 by 35, that is 7 x 5.

        7)1592   Explanation given in 1877 text:
          5)277   3 first remainder   1592 has 277 sevens and 3 ones &
            45   2 second remainder 277 sevens has 45 thirty-fives and
                                         2 sevens = 14 ones; so the true
                                         remainder is 14 + 3 = 17.

                     28) 73989745

H(s)   17. Analyze the following problems. They represent multi-
            digit problems, each in a different base. Part of the
            answers have been given to you. Using the chip trading
            till, make the exchanges needed to arrive at the correct
            answers. Then finish answering each problem in
            numerals. Indicate in which base each problem is
            written.

        This one is in base _____.   This one is in base _____.

                  2647   B70B
                +1563   - 6985
                  0 A   4 4

Red	Green	Blue	Yellow

Red	Green	Blue	Yellow

H(s)   18. On an end-of-unit assessment, second graders were
        shown two problems and were asked to circle the
        problem which would need a calculator in order to be
        solved quickly. Then they were asked to tell why they
        would use a calculator to solve the problem they circled.

```
        25                  25
      + 20                 650
                           896
                      +    106
```

Student 1 circled the first problem "besuse it is a small
prublem."

Student 2 circled the second problem "theat kas was you
pot the nabr in you pah the = and it would tall you the
asar."

Explain what experiences/activities/next steps you
would prepare for these students for tomorrow's math
class.

H(s)   19. On an end-of-unit assessment, fourth graders were
        asked

If you were given the value of each underlined digit in
dollars, which would give you the most money? Why?

1.   86,379

2.   69,873

Student 1 circled #2 "because they under line the six in
the thousands collem up there and in the ten
thousands collem down here."

Student 2 also circled #2 "I would want this one because
60,000 is more than 6,000 and 60,000 could pay for
college."

If you were to have a follow-up interview with each of
these students, what questions might you ask to further
assess their understanding of place value?

ANSWERS TO HIGHER LEVEL QUESTIONS

M(s)   2. B1 = ___22___   D3 = _836000_
           C1 = __220__   D4 = _8360000_

Technique: ___annexing zeros___

M(s)   5. 2, 4, 3, 1

M(s/v) 6. The path is as follows:

START

19683	6	9	27
5	4	3	3
18	3	5	6
6	5	3	0.9

END | 9 |

Answers will vary as students express their reasoning. Clarity of thought and expression, appropriate use of mathematical language are key points to be considered in evaluating responses.

M(v)   6. The "Tax Game" is being played in base 5 or in 5-for-1 country. Answers will vary about the questions that can be asked. Typical responses might include: "How many more blues do you need before you have a green chip?" "If you roll a six on your next turn, how many of each chip will you have when the trades are complete?" "If you have 1 green and 1 blue chip on your mat, and roll a five on the tax round, what will you do to pay your tax?"

M(v)   10. Answers will vary . This question is similar to the activity on text page 278. Student answers should be in keeping with the material presented there, although they are not limited to the example of the situational problem used there.

H (v) 12. Answers will vary. Students answers may include cultural relevance and mathematical power among the reasons for demonstrating this method.

The Russian peasant method is a <u>non-representational</u> algorithmic model. It is not based on the structure of the numeration system.

H(s/v) 13. The answer for v) is <u>1913</u>. Answers for the next portion of the problem will vary, but the <u>analysis</u> should include information similar to the following: The student is performing addition from left to right, without regard for place value. Whenever the sum of a column is 10 or greater, the child is recording the tens digit and "carrying" the ones digit to the top of the next column to the right. <u>Reteaching strategies and materials</u> might include such suggestions as: estimating the sum before doing the problem, checking to see if the student's left-to-right reading orientation is operating here, base 10 blocks, place value pocket charts or mats.

H(s)   14. The adapted algorithm answer should be:

```
         363    R 26
   27|  9827
         60
         38
         21
        172
        120
         52
         42
        107
         60
         47
         21
         26
```

H(s)   15.   23   42 | 8 9 5
             x 42

The Copy Method for both . . .

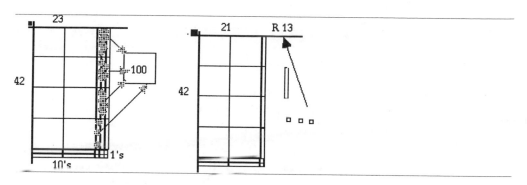

The Standard Algorithm for both . . .

H(s) 16. The adapted 1877 algorithm is:

28 | 73989745
7 | 73989745
4 | 10569963   4 first remainder
2642490   3 second remainder is 3 sevens

3 x 7 = 21 (for second remainder)
+ __4__ (from first remainder)
25 total remainder

Answer: 2642490 R 25

H(s) 17. The answers to the chip trading tills:

This one is in base <u>eleven</u> . This one is in base <u>twelve</u>

2647	B70B
+ 1563	- 6985
40AA	4946

H(v) 18. Answers will vary.

H(v) 19. Answers will vary.

P307
L(b)   1. The first concept that children must learn when working
          with rational numbers is to:
          a. reduce rationals to lowest terms
          b. key to the basic unit as the whole or one
          c. express rationals in simplest form
          d. use the circle fraction kit.

P327
L(a)   2. Which is more $\overline{.6666}$ or $\overline{.6666}$?
          a. .6666
          b. .6666
          c. Both represent the same amount in decimal fractions.
          d. Both are 1/3 of the basic building unit of wholeness.

P305
L(b)   3. The NCTM curriculum standards (1989) recommends
          that students in kindergarten through the fourth grade
          should:
          a. learn to write decimal symbols before manipulating
             concrete objects
          b. have early work that relates fractions to decimals
          c. learn decimals first and common fractions second
          d. have extensive experience with the rules involved
             with using decimals.

P306
L(d)   4. The recommended order for teaching common fractions
          is:

<u>a</u>	<u>b</u>
operations with fractions	equivalence of fractions
equivalence of fractions	partitioning of fractions
whole-to-part fractions	whole-to-part fractions
partitioning of fractions	operations with fractions

<u>c</u>	<u>d</u>
partitioning of fractions	whole-to-part fractions
whole-to-part fractions	partitioning of fractions
equivalence of fractions	equivalence of fractions
operations with fractions	operations with fractions

P338
L(a,c)   5. According to the text, when working with fractions and their operations, the field dependent learner may benefit more from using the _____.
a. Cuisenaire equivalency chart
b. multiple bars
c. fraction strip chart

P338
M(s)   6. Apply what you have learned about division of decimals to use the calculator more efficiently with this exercise. Show the correct pathway by dividing the first number by the second one as you trace your way to the ending numeral. Make only vertical and horizontal moves. No diagonals are allowed.

START

9000	9000	1000	.1
900	.01	.001	10
.1	.1	.001	.01
.001	.01	100	.1

END | 1 |

P
M(s)   7. According to Hiebert's (1987) summary of research, the following problems would not represent common understanding of school children about the relationship between _____ and _____ or between decimals and _ _____.

P316ff
M(c)   8. Which one of these answers is the most reasonable answer by using estimation, mental computation, and rounding:

4 8/12 - 7/9

a. 4 48/108
b. 5 2/3
c. 4
d. 5

P307
M(a)   9. A teacher gives the following example to her class:

The teacher says, "I divided the pizza into 6 equal pieces. Only three of my friends and I wanted a piece.

What part of the pizza was eaten? How many pieces are still left?"

The teacher is using the _____ concept of fractions.

a. whole-to-part
b. partitioning
c. equivalence
d. a and b

P320ff
M(b)   10. The following circle fraction problem models the equation:

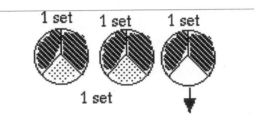

= 4 sets and 1/2 more of the next set
of 2/3

a. 3 - 2/3
b. 3 ÷ 2/3
c. 9/3 - 3/3
d. 3 x 2/3

P320
M(b)   11. If students are having trouble dividing fractions using the traditional method, which technique show below is recommended to work such problems as:

3/4 ÷ 1/2

a. 3/4 x 2/4 = 6/4 = 1 2/4 = 1 1/2

b. 3 ÷ 1   = 3 = 1 1/2
   4 ÷ 2   2

c. 3/4 x 1/2 = 3/8

d. 3/4 x 2/1 = 6/4 = 1 2/4 = 1 1/2

P306ff

M(c)   12. According to the NAEP (Mullis, 1991), more than half of
           the fourth grade students would have trouble answering
           problem. Given what you have learned in this chapter,
           explain why this might be so.

Locate 2/3 on the
   number line

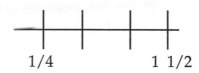

1/4   1 1/2

P325

H(s)   13. Show all the steps that would be needed in the
           traditional algorithm for adding and subtracting the two
           fractions show below, using the Cuisenaire rods. Draw
           the rods and label each with its color.

           The two fractions are: 5/6 and 1/4

P328

H(s)   14. Using the fraction strip chart, do the following
           problems, folding each strip in the appropriate places.
           Mark each strip (one per problem) as shown in the text
           and answer the questions below:

           3/4 x 5/6   2/5 ÷ 3/10

           How is the first problem read in words?

           How is the second problem read in words?

P326

H(s)   15. Using the pattern pieces named below, do all four
           operations with the fractions:

               2/3 and 1/2

           Label each operation above the manipulations shown
           for each problem.

           The patterns pieces to use are:

           the trapezoid, the hexagon, the triangle, and the blue
           rhombus

P329
H(s)   16. Add and subtract 0.43 and 0.095 using base ten blocks as decimals. Use arrows to show movement of encircled sets if exchanges are needed. Also show the total in blocks to represent the final answers for both problems. Write the decimal symbols for the actions below each example. Let the LARGE CUBE equal one whole. What will the other pieces represent?

Addition   Subtraction

P333
H(s)   17. Using graph paper, represent the regrouping needed to subtract 1.23 from 3.02. Let a 10 x 10 square = one whole unit. Write the decimal symbols for the actions.

CD
H(s)   18. In Chapter 9, the computer program, ADD, was adapted to be used with multi-digit numbers generated at random. The same explorations can be done for decimals. In Logo, if .45 + RANDOM 10 yields these possible answers:

9.45 3.45 4.45 7.45 8.45 5.45

What command would yield these answers?

-.55 .45 -4.55 -3.55

ANSWERS TO HIGHER LEVEL QUESTIONS

M(s)   7. fractions and decimals; base 10 place value system

M(v)   12. Among the explanations that can be made: emphasis on "rules" for operations before the conceptual basis of equivalence and ordering is established.

H(s)   13. All the steps that are needed to show the traditional algorithm for adding and subtracting the two fractions are shown below, using the Cuisenaire rods. Each rod should be labeled with its color.

The two fractions are: 5/6 and 1/4

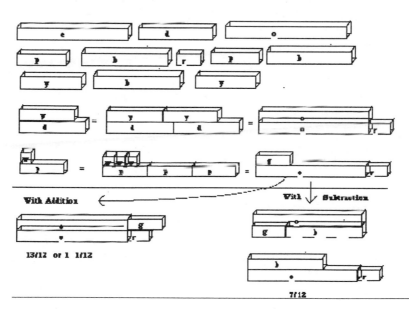

With Addition ⟵

With ↓ Subtraction

13/12 or 1 1/12

7/12

H(s)   14. Using the fraction strip chart, the problems were completed by folding each strip in the appropriate places. Each strip (one per problem) should be marked at each fold as shown on the next page:

3/4 x 5/6   2/5 ÷ 3/10

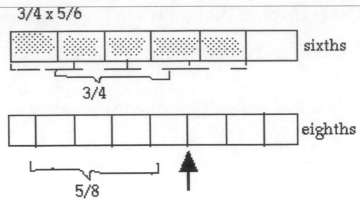

3/4 x 5/6

sixths

3/4

eighths

5/8

3/4 of 5/6 is the point on the line where 5/8 is

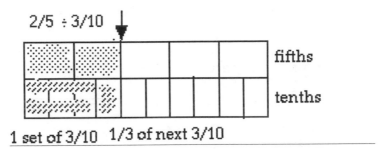

2/5 ÷ 3/10

fifths

tenths

1 set of 3/10   1/3 of next 3/10

H(s)   15. All four operations are shown using the pattern pieces
       for the fractions:

       2/3 and 1/2

The patterns pieces to use are:

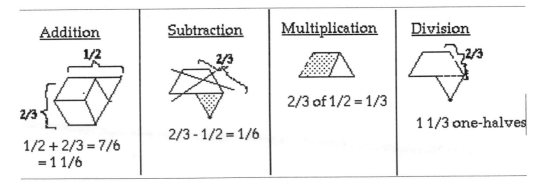

Addition	Subtraction	Multiplication	Division
1/2	2/3	2/3 of 1/2 = 1/3	2/3
2/3			
1/2 + 2/3 = 7/6 = 1 1/6	2/3 - 1/2 = 1/6		1 1/3 one-halves

H(s)   16. The regroupings needed to subtract 1.23 from 3.02 are
       shown below. The 10 x 10 square = one whole unit. The
       decimal symbols for the actions are also shown below.

```
     3.02
 -   1.23
     1.79
```

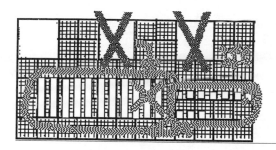

H(s) 17. The command needed is ___.45 - RANDOM 10___

No specific page is referenced. Students are being asked
to apply their knowledge of decimals in a familiar Logo
program.

H(s) 18. The following problem involving the addition and
subtraction of 0.43 and 0.095 using base ten blocks as
decimals parallels #16 above. Students can use arrows to
show the movement of encircled sets for the exchanges.
The total in blocks should be represented in the final
answers for both problems.

Addition	Subtraction
0.43	0.430
+ 0.095	- 0.095
0.525	0.335

If the LARGE CUBE is one whole, then the FLAT is one-
tenth, the LONG is 1/100, and the SMALL CUBE is
1/1000.

Thus, 0.43 will initially be represented by 4 FLATS and 3
LONGS; 0.095 will initially be shown as 9 LONGS and 5
SMALL CUBES. It is important in the subtraction
problem that only 0.43 is modeled. 0.095 should be taken
away from 0.43.

CD
L(c)   1. Use a calculator to find the percent of arrows which
              missed the target.

Total Shots	Shots Missing Target	% Hitting Target
1960	1375	?

              The answer is:
              a. 99.298469 %
              b. 0.7015306 %
              c. 29.84694 %
              d. 70.15306 %

CD
L(d)   2. Which Logo commands made these ratios?

              a. HEX 2 OCT 3
                 PENT 6 STAR 7
              b. 1PART OCT 3 HEX 2
                 2PART STAR 7 PENT 6
              c. 1PART OCT 3 1PART STAR 7
                 2PART HEX 2 2PART PENT 6
              d. 1PART OCT 3 2PART HEX 2
                 1PART STAR 7 2PART PENT 6

P352ff
L(c)   3. The Logo drawings in the preceding test item are an
              example of:
              a. two equivalent ratios
              b. two equivalent proportions
              c. two non-equivalent ratios
              d. two non-equivalent proportions

P356
L(a)   4. A statement of equality between two ratios is known as a

              _____
              a. proportion
              b. rate
              c. ratio
              d. percent

P348
L(d)   5. A ratio to 100 is also known as a _____

a. proportion
b. rate
c. ratio
d. percent

P352ff

M(v) 6. Both ratio and rate involve a comparison between two quantities. How would you answer the student in your class who asks, "How can I tell a ratio from a rate?"

CD

M(a) 7. Analyze the following procedure adapted from the program in Chapter 11 on the CD. Name the procedure as it should appear on the first line.

_____?_____
HT
REPEAT 36 [FD 1 RT 10 * .005]
END

The procedure should be named:
a. TO .5%CIRCLE
b. TO 5/1000 %CIRCLE
c. TO .005%CIRCLE
d. TO .05%CIRCLE

P356

M(v) 8. Use graph paper and sketch an example of application of ratio as practiced in ancient Egypt.

P351

M(s) 9. Shade 25% of the star below.

P360

M(b) 10. Which type of learner may benefit more from the activity in question #9 as discussed in the text?
a. field dependent learner
b. field independent learner
c. tactile learner
d. auditory learner

CD

M(b) 11. Reading from left to right, the Logo commands that made these drawings were FLAG .125 FLAG .25 FLAG .3333 FLAG .50 FLAG .75 FLAG 1. The missing flag is a third smaller than the last flag on the right and 8.333 % smaller than the next largest flag by its side.

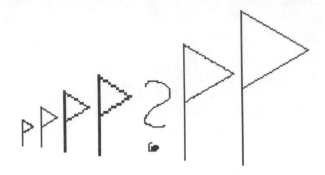

Which set of procedures will make the missing flag?

a	b
FD -7.583 * 60 REPEAT 3 [FD -7.583 * 60 RT 120]	FD .6666 * 60 REPEAT 3 [FD .6666 * 60 RT 120]
c	d
FD .3333333 * 60 REPEAT 3 [FD .3333333 * 60]	FD .625 * 60 REPEAT 3 [FD .625 * 60 RT 120]

P356

M(d)

12. Using the Logo flags in the preceding question, numbering the seven flag positions from left to right:

$$\frac{\text{Flag \#1}}{\text{Flag \#2}} \quad = \quad \frac{\text{Flag \#4}}{\text{Flag \#7}}$$

The relationship between the flags above represents:
a. two equivalent ratios
b. two non-equivalent ratios
c. a true proportion
d. a and c

P348ff

M(b)

13. Which decimal and percent represents the same number as forty-three millionths?
a. 0.00000043 and 0.000043 %
b. 0.000043 and 0.0043 %
c. 0.0000043 and 0.00043 %
d. 0.40003 and 0.0403 %

P350

M(c)

14. According to the fourth mathematics assessment of the national assessment of education progress (Kouba et al., 1988), which of the following problems were unable to

be answered by the majority of middle school students (age 13)?

  a. $0.9 = 9/10$
  b. $0.25\% = 1/4$
  c. $0.9 = 90\%$

CD
H(v)   15. Use the ad below to create a situational problem that will use <u>either</u> discount and percent of decrease <u>or</u> selling price and percent of increase. Use your calculator to find the answers to your problems.

Santa's Helpers

For Budget Headaches

Reminiscing – The Game for People Over 30	$14.95
Planters 3-Can Holiday Gift Pack	$ 5.48
M&M Holiday Bags	$ 1.99
Rolo Color Coloring Desk	$ 9.95
Panasonic Smooth Operator	$42.95
Diet Coke 16 oz. - 6-pack	$ 1.88
Pro R50 Hair Dryer	$11.99

CD
H(v)   16. Create a problem situation involving the relationship of decimals to percents that students could appropriately use a spreadsheet to solve. Sketch the spreadsheet program.

P362
H(v)   17. A student solve the problem:

> "A shirt is marked down 30 %. If the original price was $5.98, what will you pay for it on sale?"

by writing $5.98 - .30 = $5.68.

Analyze the student's error. Describe the process you would encourage the student to use to arrive at a correct solution.

P356ff
H(v)   18. Using graph paper, represent a proportion that has as its common ratio 4 : 5. Write the decimal and percent equivalents of the common ratio.

H(v)   19. Use the base ten blocks to show the decimal
            representation for the common fraction of 1/8. The
            tenths have been drawn for you. Show the regroupings
            needed. Finally, show the relationship between the
            decimal representation of 1/8 and its percent equivalent.

H(v)   20. As part of her alternative assessment program, Ms.
            Azwell presented the following situation in an
            interview setting to each of her sixth graders:

> The Nelson's bill at Applebee's came to $38.00. Mr.
> Nelson took out $40 to pay. Will he need more money
> to leave a 15% tip? Explain your answer.

Design a rubric or scoring guide to evaluate the
responses and then score the following actual student
responses.

Student 1: Well, 15% is .15 and 38 x .15 is (worked it out
on paper) $5.70. Yes, he will because 15% of $38 is $5.70.
Therefore he would need $3.70 more money.

Student 2: Uh, can I do this part on paper (40 x .15)? Ok,
that's .06. He will need 4 more doller to leave a 15% tip.

Student 3: See, 15% of $38 is 5.70 (working it out on
paper) and 35 + 5/70 is $43.70. Yes, Mr. Nelson will need
more money. A 15% tip of a $38 bill is $5.70. If $5.70 is
added to the bill of $38, the total bill will come to $43.70.
The $40 he has is not enough to pay the bill. he will
need $3.70 more.

== Cover Up Next Portion When Copying Test ==

ANSWERS TO HIGHER LEVEL QUESTIONS

M(v)   6. Answers may vary, but the college student should clearly
           indicate the student understands that rate involve a
           *certain magnitude, element, or quantity compared in
           relation to a unit of something else.* (Text page 360 &
           CD)

M(v)   8. Answers may vary. A scale for drawing an enlargement would be a typical response here.

M(s)   9. The quarter region the student chooses to shade may vary, but the shading should extend for a full quarter of the star.

H(v)   15. Answers will vary.

H(v)   16. Answers will vary.

H(v)   17. Answers will vary, but in general, students will indicate that this child appears to be thinking of percent as money and is subtracting, rather than finding the percentage and then subtracting from the original price. An estimation process such as that described in this chapter is an appropriate method to encourage the child to use.

H(v)   18. Answers will vary, but the drawings should be in the required ratio.

H(v)   19. The decimal representation for the common fraction of 1/8:

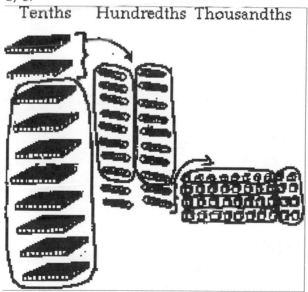

Its percent equivalent: 12 1/2% or 12/5%.

No page number is referenced. Students are applying their understanding of the relationships between common fractions, decimals, and percents using a concrete manipulative.

H(v)   20. Answers will vary. The rubric or scoring guide should
             consider the essential elements of the task, the strategy
             or procedure, and the reasonableness of the explanation.
             They should be able to justify their ratings based on the
             criteria of the rubric.

TEST QUESTIONS -- CHAPTER 13

P383
L(c)
1. A set of numbers both positive, negative and zero defines the:
   a. number system
   b. numeration
   c. integers
   d. whole numbers

P383
M(s)
2. A postman takes away 6 bills for $5 each. Write the number sentence which represents the story.

P369
L(a)
3. According to the NCTM curriculum standards (1989), looking for patterns in mathematics is the essence of _.
   a. inductive reasoning
   b. deductive reasoning
   c. transductive reasoning
   d. egocencratic behavior

P379
L(d)
4. The mollusk shell pictured below shows 21 chambers which become larger in an increasing spiral. Each chamber is the size of the two chambers which come directly before it when the two preceding chambers are added together. This describes the number pattern known as:

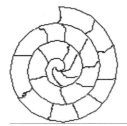

   a. Pascal's triangle
   b. Pythagorean triplets
   c. Figurate numbers
   d. Fibonacci sequence

P373
M(b)
5. The Sieve of Eratosthenes method of finding prime numbers would be more likely to benefit the _____.

a. field dependent learner
b. field independent learner
c. both a and b
d. middle school student

P374
L(c)
6. If the least non-zero number of two counting numbers is a multiple of both numbers, then it is the _____ .
a. GCF
b. GCD
c. LCM
d. a and b

P378ff
M(c)
7. Who should really be credited with the Pythagorean Theorem? _____ and Pascal's Triangle? _____
a. Greek mathematicians; French mathematicians
b. Pythagoras; Blaise Pascal
c. African mathematicians; Asian mathematicians
d. Aristotle; Pierre Fermat

M(v)
8. Why is it important to "give credit where credit is due" in situations such as that in question #7 above?

P386
M(s)
9. Show how students might use Cuisenaire rods to find solutions for the equation $2x + 3y = 9$

P389ff
M(s)
10. Use a table to show solutions for the equation $x - 3y = -6$

P390
M(s)
11. On the coordinate axes below, graph the equations in #9 and #10 above. Identify the solution set of the pair of equations.

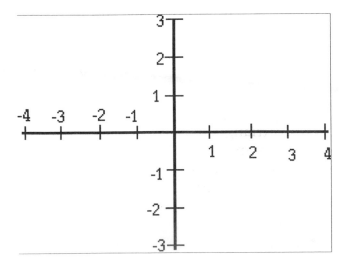

12. From your work in the text and the CD with the Sieve of Eratosthenes, what will happen to the multiples of three numbers in the second 100 numbers of the Sieve?
   a. The number of multiples of three numbers will decrease.
   b. The number of multiples of three numbers will increase.
   c. The number of multiples of three numbers will stay the same.
   d. The number of multiples of three numbers will no longer exist.

13. If all the numerals were filled in the blanks, the numerals on the nth level would add up to:

```
                        1
                 1             1
              1       2       1
           1     3       3      1
         1    4     6     4     1
       1   5    10    10    5    1
      1   6   15   20   15   6   1
    1   7  21  35    35   21   7   1
   1   8   28 56   70    56  28  8   1
  1  9  36  84  126  126  84  36  9  1

          .
          .
          .
   1 n                            n 1
```

   a. n^2
   b. 2^n
   c. Four times the total of level n - 2
   d. b and c

14. When assessing students' ability to identify and extend patterns at the middle school level, which of the following questions is likely to be most helpful?
   a. Did you ask the others in your group how they found the pattern?
   b. Why don't you try adding 1 and multiplying by 3?

c. Look at what you described for finding the 2nd term and the third. In what way is the 4th term like that.

d. Why didn't you get "13" for the 4th term?

P375ff

M(s)   15. Below are the prime towers for two numbers:

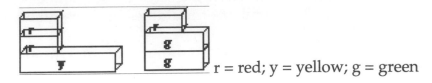

r = red; y = yellow; g = green

The choices are . . .
#1. one red and one green rod
#2. one red rod
#3. 2 red rods, 2 green rods, and 1 yellow rod
#4. 1 red, 1 green, and 1 yellow rod

In rods the LCM is _____ and the GCF is _____ .

P376

M(0)   16. Check the divisibility of the dividend below by 2, 5, 10,. 4, 8, 3, and 9. Two are not possible. Change the ones digit in the dividend so it will be divisible by the two divisors not possible here. It must also be divisible by the original five.

$$\overline{\rule{2cm}{0pt}}$$

⌐ 94964406489

P373

M(c)   17. Using the Sieve of Eratosthenes for the prime number 17, when is the first time a multiple of 17, greater than 17, will be crossed out for the first time without a smaller prime as its multiple?
a. 34
b. 187
c. 289
d. Not enough information to tell

P391

H(v)   18. Examine the following sequence and determine which number does not fit the pattern   12   21   34   43   56   65   67   87
Explain why the number doesn't belong in the sequence and tell what the correct number would be. What would be the next pair of numbers in this sequence? How did you determine this?

P374

H(s)   19. The division algorithm below has only one correct
       answer. It is possible to place the correct numerals in the
       blanks with only 4 numerals showing. What you have
       learned about divisibility rules, factors, and multiples
       should help you.

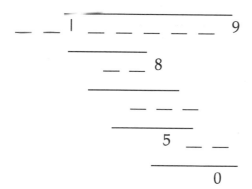

P376

H(v)   20. The ending exercises of Chapter 13 asked you to find the
       divisibility rule for 11. State in your own words the
       reasoning behind the rule which will always work for
       the base ten number system. Test several numbers to
       prove your reasoning. Remember number theory, as
       discussed in Chapter 13, is based on patterns in number
       relationships.

H(v)   21. On an end of the year assessment, sixth graders were
       asked to solve the following problems. Analyze the
       student responses and describe what they understand, or
       do not understand, about the using variables in solving
       equations.

> The 6th grade vs. faculty basketball game charged $1.00
> for students and $1.50 for adults. Three times as many
> students as adults attended the game. If 300 people paid
> to attend the game, how many students attended, how
> many adults attended, and how much money was
> raised?
>
> Write an algebraic equation and solve for X.

Student 1:   3n x n = 300

$$\frac{4n}{4} = \frac{300}{4}$$

n = 75

# of adults = 75 = $450
# of students = 225 = $225
amount of money $625

Student 2: 3n + n = 300   # of adults = 50 = $75
$$\frac{4n}{4} = 300$$ # of students = 150 = 150
                                                              $225
amount of money = $225

Student 3:   III. Procedure
    1. find the No. of adults and children
    2. Use x for the unknown

        x + 3x = 300

                                        1
        300      $\frac{300}{4}$ $\frac{4x}{4x}$

    x = 75 adults
    3x = 225 students

Take 300 - 75 = 225

IV Solution
    There was 225 students.
    They raised $337.50.
    There was 75 adults.

== Cover Up Next Portion When Copying Test ==

ANSWERS TO HIGHER LEVEL QUESTIONS

M(s)   2. $^-6\,x\,^-5 = {}^+30$

M(v)   8. Answers will vary, but responses should clearly indicate
        that the college students understand and appreciate the
        contributions of other cultures and the importance of
        instilling that appreciation in their elementary and
        middle school students.

M(v)   9. It is expected that since the equation has 2 unknowns the
        college students will show more than 1 solution. Two

solutions would be: a) 3 red rods and 1 green rod are equivalent to a blue rod and b) 3 green rods are equivalent to a blue rod; that is x = 0 , or no other rods are needed.

M(v)   10. Again answers may vary, but it is expected that the table will be set up in the following way:

X	Y
-6	0
-3	1
0	2
3	3

M(s)   11. The solution set for the two equations is (1, 2 1/3). The graph on the coordinate axis must be as shown below:

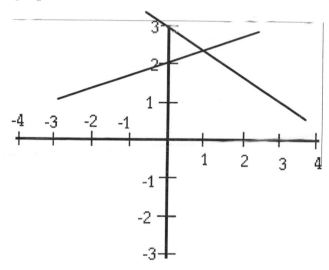

H(v)   18. 67 does not belong in this sequence. It should be 78. The remaining portion of the answers may vary -- One way the sequence can be formed is by pairing consecutive digits (12) and then reversing them (21). If students remain with two digit numbers, the next pair of numbers would be (90) and (09).
If students see the sequence as formed by alternately adding 9 (12 + 9 = 21) and then 13 (21 + 13 = 34), the next pair of numbers would be (100) and (109).

19. The correct answer is:

$$
\begin{array}{r}
1\ 7\ 1\ 9 \\
61\ |\ \overline{1\ 0\ 4\ 8\ 5\ 9} \\
\underline{6\ 1} \\
4\ 3\ 8 \\
\underline{4\ 2\ 7} \\
1\ 1\ 5 \\
\underline{6\ 1} \\
5\ 4\ 9 \\
\underline{5\ 4\ 9} \\
0
\end{array}
$$

20. The following line of reasoning should be seen for the divisibility rule for 11:

Since the rule is for base ten numbers, one can look for a pattern with base ten numbers where divisibility by 11 would exist. Two such patterns can be seen:

With Base Ten		Test	Is it divisible?
$10 = 11 - 1$	and	11/11	YES
$100 = 101 - 1$	and	101/11	NO
$1000 = 1001 - 1$	and	1001/11	YES
$10000 = 10001 - 1$	and	10001/11	NO

etc.

$10 = 9 + 1$	and	9/11	NO
$100 = 99 + 1$	and	99/11	YES
$1000 = 999 + 1$	and	999/11	NO
$10000 = 9999 + 1$	and	9999/11	YES

etc.

Note that divisibility alternates in each pattern, and that both patterns must be used together to insure that every possibility for divisibility has the chance to be answered in the affirmative. Also, the operations of addition and subtraction are needed. Therefore, if alternating digits are added together and their sums are subtracted from one another, all possibilities would have been checked. If the resulting answer is divisible by 11, then the entire number is divisible by 11. Since our number system builds in place value from right to left, the alternating digits should start from right to left also. The smaller set of numbers should be taken from the larger set so the answer is always a positive counting number to be tested for divisibility.

Examples with base ten numbers:

240182613 ==> (3 + 6 + 8 + 0 + 2) = 19
               (1 + 2 + 1 + 4)   = 8
                              11 and 11/11 is divisible

897841235684 ==>   (4 + 6 + 3 + 1 + 8 + 9) = 31
                   (8 + 5 + 2 + 4 + 7 + 8) = 34
                                    3 and 3/11
                                    is NOT
divisible

H(v)   21. Answers will vary but students should note that some get the right answer for the wrong reason ... there is perhaps more emphasis on rote rules than on understanding the concept.

P411

L(b)   1. A graph which is used to show various data that involve variation is called:
    a. a circle graph
    b. a box-and-whisker plot
    c. a continuous graph
    d. a bar graph

P409

L(c)   2. When the interpretation of data gives the fractional part of each quantity to the whole, a _____ should be used to show the results.
    a. scatter graph
    b. scale
    c. circle graph
    d. proportional line graph

P412

L(d)   3. Which of the following is an example of data analysis practiced by early civilizations?
    a. levying taxes in Egypt
    b. development of geometric formulas in Mesopotamia
    c. prediction of eclipses by the Mayans
    d. all of the above

P422ff

L(c)   4. The number of objects placed in an arrangement with no distinct order is called _____ and the formula that is used to determine the number is _____ .
    a. probability; $P(X\ Y)$
    b. statistics; $P(A \mid B)$
    c. permutations; $_nP_x$
    d. combinations; $_nC_x$

P424

M(136) 5. Look at the seating chart on the next page. How many different seating arrangements can be made for the girls if the teacher wants them to sit in pairs? The teacher is willing to change the room arrangement. You may use a calculator.

Row 1	Ann	Sally	Lou	Jean	
Row 2	Jane	Jan			
Row 3	Janet	Sue	Mabel	Shelly	Marge
Row 4	Esther				
Row 5					
Row 6	Liz	Ann	Shirley	Joan	Meg

P407

M(b)

6. The continuous graph below shows the record of weight for humans as they grow older. The X-axis stands for _____ while the Y-axis stands for _____.

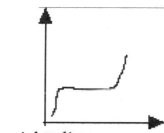

a. weight; distance
b. age; weight
c. age; distance
d. weight; age

P415ff

M(b)

7. Using three dice, what is the probability that three fives will be tossed on any one roll?
a. 1/36
b. 1/216
c. 1/18
d. 1/54

P410

M(v)

8. Label the X and Y axes with appropriate labels and write a brief narrative using the data provided.

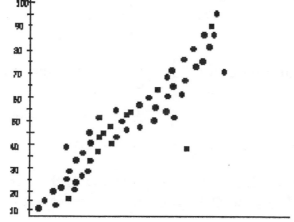

P422ff

M(720) 9. The PE teacher plans a set of 10 races. At the end of the
races the 10 winners will compete for the gold, silver,
and bronze award in one big race all together. How
many ways can the medals be awarded to these top
athletes?

P403

M(a) 10. Which graph(s) below give(s) the accurate
representation of the following information?
There are 24 students in the class who like ice
cream best. Twelve students like cake best.
Eighteen students like spaghetti best. Six students
like apples best. Eighteen students like pizza best.

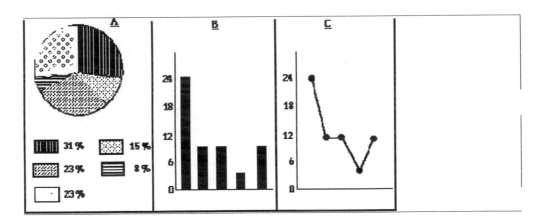

a. Graph A
b. Graph B
c. Graph C
d. b and c

P406ff

M(Yes) 11. Do Graphs B and C depict the same data (not necessarily
the data in the problem)?

P406ff

M(No) 12. Would a typical 4th grade student be able to read the
data from both graphs (B and C) easily and accurately?

P406ff

H(v) 13. Justify your answer for #12 above. How might the
interpretations of the two graphs differ?

P406ff

M(v) 14. Take the data from problem #10 above and organize it
into a bar graph, a line graph, and finally a picture graph.

P406ff

H(v) 15. In what ways does your interpretation of the data gain
or lose understanding as you look at first one graph and

then another? What advantages does one graph have over the others?

P412
&CD

H(s)   16. Using the Cuisenaire arrangement shown below, make the exchanges needed to show how the mean of the distribution is found in the physical movement of the rods. Draw the end result of the exchanges.

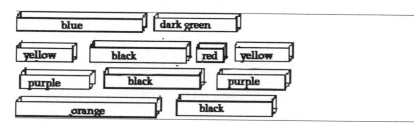

H(v)   17. Here is a problem on a sixth grade end-of-year assessment. Read the problem, develop a rubric or scoring guide for it, and then rate the responses of the students. Are there any significant misconceptions? If so, what teaching steps would you take next to address them?

> Suppose you and four of your friends called your own dentist (each one of you goes to a different dentist) to ask what sugarless gum he or she would recommend. <u>None</u> of them recommend Sugarless Chewy Gum. If 4 out of 5 dentists surveyed in a national poll of 1,000 dentists did recommend Sugarless Chewy Gum, how would you explain to someone that the poll could still be accurate?

<u>Student 1</u>: You can say that the national poll was accurate because they polled more people. Then, they have a greater chance than just taking four dentists.

<u>Student 2</u>: Because it was a national survey. That means the took the opinion of many dentist. If 1000 were surveyed only 800 recommended Sugarless Chewy Gum. The total is acutlly an average

<u>Student 3</u>: It is just the same as saying 999 dentists out of 1000 recommend it.

<u>Student 4</u>: If there were 1000 dentists surveyed, there would be 200 groups of 5. 4 out of 5 said "yes" they did

recommend Sugarless Chewy Gum, but 1 out of 5 didn't. This would leave 200 dentists who <u>didn't</u> recommend Sugarless Chewy Gum and 4 friend's dentist could be among them.

<u>Student 5</u>: I don't know how I would explain it to someone if I don't understand it myself. Maybe, because 5 is more than 1000 so 5 isn't really going to make a difference.

== Cover Up Next Portion When Copying Test ==

ANSWERS TO HIGHER LEVEL QUESTIONS

M(v)　8. Answers will vary. The titles chosen for the axes should be in keeping with the written narrative.

H(v)　13. In general, elementary students have more difficulty interpreting line graphs. College students' responses should clearly indicate to the instructor their understanding of the problems students have interpreting line graphs, as found in the text page 407.

M(v)　14. Answers will vary, inasmuch as students choose different unit representations.

H(v)　15. Answer will vary. Students should clearly organize and label their responses so that the particular graphs being discussed are apparent.

H(s)　16. The students should see that it is best to exchange the large rods first. Such as: exchange the 3 black rods for 3 dark green rods and 3 white rods. Exchange the blue rod for a dark green rod and 3 more white rods. Exchange the orange rod for a dark green rod and 4 white rods. Use the white rods to add to the small rods to bring them to the same length as the dark green rods. The final exchange should show all the rods exchanged for the dark green rods. There should be a line of eleven dark green rods, proving the mean is the dark green rod.

H(v)　17. Answers will vary, but the essential elements of the task ... interpreting the data and developing reasonable explanations of the variances from the data should be part of the rubric or scoring guide.

NOTES

NOTES

NOTES

NOTES